HÖLDERLIN

THE
SEAGULL
LIBRARY OF
GERMAN
LITERATURE

This publication has been supported by a grant from
the Goethe-Institut India

Seagull Books, 2019

Originally published as *Hölderlin—Stück in zwei Akten* by Peter Weiss

© Suhrkamp Verlag, Frankfurt am Main, 1971

First published in English by Seagull Books, 2010

English translation © Jon Swan and Carl Weber

ISBN 978 0 8574 2 713 7

British Library Cataloguing-in-Publication Data
A catalogue record for this book is available from the British Library

Typeset by Seagull Books, Calcutta, India
Printed and bound by WordsWorth India, New Delhi, India

HÖLDERLIN

A PLAY IN TWO ACTS

PETER WEISS

WITH AN AFTERWORD BY THE AUTHOR

TRANSLATED BY JON SWAN,
IN COLLABORATION WITH CARL WEBER

INTRODUCTION BY ROBERT COHEN

Seagull
B O O K S

LONDON NEW YORK CALCUTTA

CONTENTS

INTRODUCTION

'Our illnesses are mostly political illnesses. When our breathing stops, when the blood clots in the veins, the heart fails, then our weariness has settled in the organism, and we react with our whole person as a unit, as a natural process, react definitively to a situation that can no longer be dealt with rationally.' This perceptive description of a psychosomatic illness appears in the notations in which Peter Weiss tried to come to terms with the defeat he suffered with his play *Trotsky in Exile*. Its opening on 20 January 1970 in Düsseldorf was a disaster. The Left—the only conceivable audience for such a play during the cold war— and especially the students radicalized in 1968, detested it. For the communist German Democratic Republic (GDR), which considered Weiss an important ally, a play about Trotsky in the year commemorating Lenin's one-hundredth birthday was heretical. The GDR let the dramatist know that he was no longer welcome. On 6 June 1970, a few weeks after he had written the above lines, Weiss's breathing would indeed stop, the blood would clot in his veins, his heart would fail. The following day, in the hospital, he noted that his cardiac arrest had occurred 'incredibly suddenly, absolutely unexpectedly'.

It can indeed seem unexpected that the dramatist whose play *Marat/Sade* had only a few short years before become a huge international success reached such a low point. Peter Weiss was born in Berlin in 1916 to a Czech father of Jewish origin and a Swiss-German mother. He was studying painting when the Nazis came to power in 1933. The family left for London in 1935, then moved to Czechoslovakia, before finally settling in Sweden in 1939. During the war years Weiss led the life of a bohemian painter with little success and almost no income. In 1946 he became a Swedish citizen (Weiss never acquired German citizenship). With his painting receiving hardly any recognition, he started writing in Swedish, as well as in German. Just like his painting of this period, his written work was influenced by Surrealism, an influence he shared with *Fyrtiotalisterna*, a group of Swedish painters and writers of his generation. Hesitating between Swedish and German, he wrote lyrical and nearly hermetic texts, which for the most part he could not get published. In the early 1950s he turned to filmmaking. A series of Surrealist and experimental short films was followed by several documentaries that, for the first time, focused Weiss' attention towards the real world, its social and economic conditions. All this artistic activity seemed to go nowhere until in 1959 the prestigious West German Suhrkamp Verlag published a Weiss text from 1952 with the oddly inelegant title *The Shadow of the Body of the Coachman* (*Der Schatten des Körpers des Kutschers*). It was followed in short order by two works of autobiographical fiction, *Leavetaking* (*Abschied von den Eltern*) and *Vanishing Point* (*Fluchtpunkt*). With the success and recognition these publications brought him, Weiss abruptly stopped painting and filmmaking and became a German-language author. He had written several small plays when, in the early 1960s, he turned to the French Revolution and wrote a play about one of its protagonists, Jean-Paul Marat. His dramatic counterpart was to be the Marquis de Sade, long an icon of the Surrealists. The play, which opened at the Schiller Theater West Berlin on 29 April 1964, drew enormous attention, not only for its sensational content, but also through its title: *The Persecution and Assassination of Jean-Paul Marat as Performed by the Inmates of the Asylum of Charenton Under the Direction of Monsieur de Sade* (*Die Verfolgung und Ermordung Jean Paul Marats dargestellt durch die Schauspielgruppe des Hospizes zu Charenton unter Anleitung des Herrn de Sade*). It became a worldwide success with Peter Brook's London staging at the Aldwych Theater in the fall of 1964 and with a filmed version, also directed by Brook, in 1967.

This opulent play was followed by a work that was radically devoid of all theatricality and drained of all entertainment value. It consisted of nothing but the monotonous voices of the perpetrators and survivors of the Auschwitz death camp. *The Investigation* (*Die Ermittlung*) opened on 19 October 1965, simultaneously on 16 stages in both West and East Germany—the only such event to unite the two countries in a common enterprise. Much debated and contested to this day, the play cemented Weiss's aura as one of the most important dramatists of his time. Radicalized by his work on the French Revolution and the Nazi genocide, Weiss joined the Swedish (Euro-) Communist Party (*Vänsterpartiet kommunisterna*, VPK). In quick succession he wrote two plays about the effects of colonialism and imperialism on the so-called Third World: *Song of the Lusitanian Bogey* (*Gesang vom lusitanischen Popanz*, 1967) about the Portuguese colony of Angola, and *Viet Nam Discourse* (*Viet Nam Diskurs*, 1968). These highly stylized works were intended to intervene in the ongoing struggles for liberation both in Angola and in Vietnam. Their reception did not come close to the success of the plays that had preceded them. *Viet Nam Discourse* was followed by the play on Trotsky that eventually led to Weiss' breakdown.

'Our illnesses are mostly political illnesses.' Was the mental illness from which the great German poet Friedrich Hölderlin (1770–1843) suffered over the last four decades of his life a 'political illness'? The book in which Peter Weiss found such an interpretation of Hölderlin's malady was published in 1969: Pierre Bertaux's *Hölderlin und die Französische Revolution* (Hölderlin and the French Revolution)—a painstakingly researched and elegantly written study in which the French Germanist seeks to set the record straight. Traditionally viewed as a pious and ecstatic poet of a mythological ancient Greece and revered by Nazi ideologues, Hölderlin through Bertaux's reinterpretation becomes a radical German Jacobin whose thinking is profoundly affected by events in France. Hölderlin's works are shown to be saturated with the ideas of the French Revolution—ideas of freedom, equality, brotherhood, and even of tyrannicide. Until the publication of Bertaux's monograph there had been no significant effort to correct the image of Hölderlin promoted by the Nazis. An essay on Hölderlin by Marxist philosopher Georg Lukács had had no impact, and neither had the research on Hölderlin by Germanists in East Germany. Only when Weiss' *Hölderlin*, equally indebted to Bertaux's study and to Lukács' essay, was presented on stages in the Federal Republic could the reactionary image of Hölderlin no longer be maintained.

Still reeling from the defeat he had suffered with the Trotsky play, Weiss began working on the Hölderlin material. It brought back childhood memories. In 1928 12-year-old Weiss had spent several months in the southern German city of Tübingen, where he stayed with an aunt who was married to a lawyer called Autenrieth. The Autenrieth house was located on the banks of the Neckar River directly beside the tower in which, a hundred years earlier, the mentally ill poet had spent the last four decades of his life. Uncle Autenrieth, as Weiss became aware only much later, was a descendant of the infamous Professor Autenrieth who had so badgered Hölderlin in the name of science.

The tower as a place of confinement and oppression had been the topic of Weiss' first play, *The Tower* (1948). At the time, it was a metaphor for Weiss' own traumatic childhood; now, it became the place where a great poet had languished for decades into his old age. Starting with this image, Weiss drafted a play in the spring of 1970; on 22 May he was already reading parts of it to his publisher, Siegfried Unseld. After the heart attack, work continued in the hospital; by mid-June the order of the scenes had been determined. When Weiss left the hospital in late July, however, it became clear to him that he did not yet have the strength to carry out such intense work. Instead, he began writing an extensive diary, in which he once again tried to come to an understanding of the pain and the obsessions of his life and oeuvre, his difficult youth, his stay with the Autenrieths, as well as of issues such as the relationship between art and society, the Third World, the depressing experiences with *Trotsky in Exile*, and his political commitment. What is apparent in these notes, which were published several years after Weiss' death under the title *Rekonvaleszenz* (Reconvalescence), is a new validation of the unconscious, of fantasies, dreams, visions, and hallucinations for artistic work. This sphere had been the focus of Weiss's early artistic production. In the 1960s, Weiss' growing attention to the political demands of the day had overwhelmed these preoccupations. Now, however, with the renewed awareness of the fragility of his own body, with the awareness of how easily and permanently everything could have ended, he began to revalue the irrational, the emotional.

Gradually, in the fall of 1970, work on *Hölderlin* resumed, and in late 1970 a first version was sent to the publisher. The premiere took place on 18 September 1971, in Stuttgart, under the direction of Peter Palitzsch. It was followed by numerous stagings in West Germany, Switzerland, and the GDR that were greeted by accolades as well as intense criticism since Weiss had dared to revise the image of one of the great figures of German culture.

For academic philologists and literary critics, especially the more conservative among them, the play represented a radical rupture with the traditional image of Hölderlin. Had Weiss interpreted the facts irresponsibly? Had the historical Hölderlin been misrepresented? For a better understanding of Weiss' representation of the great poet one needs to look at the aesthetic concepts of the play, as well as at its themes and obsessions.

Like *Trotsky in Exile*, *Hölderlin* presents a biography of the title figure as a two-act drama, divided here into a prologue, eight scenes, and an epilogue. Scenes 1–7 dramatize events from Hölderlin's life in the period 1793–1807. Scene 8 sums up the remaining almost forty years until Hölderlin's death. The action unfolds chronologically. At the beginning of each scene a singer announces the time and place. There is a renewed opulence of theatrical means

—choruses, song and dance, a singing herald, dreamlike and nightmarish scenes and visions, as well as a short play-within-the-play. As a theatre of the senses, *Hölderlin* is a successor to *Marat/Sade*, which can be taken quite literally. *Hölderlin* begins where *Marat/Sade* ends, on 14 July 1793, the day after the death of Jean-Paul Marat, whose murder is gloatingly announced at the beginning of *Hölderlin* by Duke Karl Eugen von Württemberg. The play's closeness to *Marat/Sade* is underscored also in the obsessive portrayal of scenes of torture and ecstasy which once again serve as a reminder that, as the Marquis de Sade puts it in the earlier play, this is a 'world of bodies'. Scenes of torture recur repeatedly in *Hölderlin*—for instance, when the rebellious student Sinclair is given a thrashing while Hölderlin weeps (scene 1); when Hölderlin is brought forth in a straitjacket and face mask and force-fed (Scene 7); or when he conjures up an image during the crossing the Vendee, 'where the earth screamed of corpses / and with each step in the field / I stumbled against skulls and bones'—a horrific image that Weiss had first created in a 1946 drawing 'Adam, Eva, und Kain' (Adam, Eve and Cain) and which he had also used in *Marat/Sade*.

The ecstasy of the body is conjured up in the scene where the emancipated Wilhelmine Kirms opens her dress and invites Hölderlin to an erotic encounter—an anachronistic moment, for in Hölderlin's time liberated sexuality was as little to be had as equality of women. Startled, Hölderlin declines. Having pined away in a hopeless and Platonic love for Susette Gontard, who is wasting away as the wife of a Frankfurt banker, he is unable to become an equal partner to the self-confident Kirms, to her combative feminism and her contempt for this weakly 'sex / along with what dangles/between their legs'. Under the sexual taboos of the bourgeoisie, the promise of ecstasy turns into torment. This was in many ways Weiss' own obsession, his childhood having been traumatized by such torment; he had recreated it over and over in his early work. In *Hölderlin* this torment is suffered by young Fritz von Kalb. For nights on end Hölderlin must watch over him to prevent him from succumbing to his 'vice'. It is an agonizing duty, since Hölderlin himself is a victim of the taboos of society and its 'ice-cold zone of the prevailing order'. Sobbing hysterically, he starts slapping Fritz, who is masturbating.

The repression and oppression that permeate scenes like these are not limited to the sexual sphere. In a disturbingly convincing scene, both Hölderlin and Fritz slap themselves. This is an expression of self-hatred that has always characterized the victims of repression—and has always benefited the oppressors. A painful image, and one that Weiss had used once before, in *Leavetaking*, where the maid, Augusta, humiliated by the narrator's mother, slaps herself in the face.

From today's perspective Weiss' play alone cannot explain the heated controversy over whether or not *Hölderlin* 'correctly' represents the great poet and contemporary of Goethe and Schiller. The debate appears as a rearguard action. *Hölderlin* was part of a reorientation in the humanities that had emerged in the Federal Republic as a consequence of the student revolt of 1968. Weiss was not the only writer who by then was rejecting the antiquated image of the poet. In 1970, a year before *Hölderlin* opened, a biographical radio play about Hölderlin by GDR author Stephan Hermlin, titled *Scardanelli*, was broadcast in the GDR. Also in the GDR, in 1976, Gerhard Wolf's revisionist *Der arme Hölderlin* was published. That same year Peter

Härtling's biographical novel *Hölderlin*, in which Peter Weiss's play is mentioned as one of the sources, appeared in West Germany.

Unlike *Viet Nam Discourse*, the play about Hölderlin is not foremost a presentation of facts. The transformation of factual material into an aesthetic artifact is signaled from the very beginning when Hölderlin speaks about himself in the third person in a manner recalling Brechtian distanciation. The figure of the singer, the surreal scenes of ecstasy and of torture, Hölderlin's visionary fantasies, the meeting with Karl Marx—an invention of Weiss—all signal a free and fictionalized treatment. As does the complex disruption of chronological time, particularly in the play-within-a-play about Empedócles. All of these aesthetic and dramatic devices, themes, and motifs remove Weiss' play from a narrowly historiographical representation of reality. They allow the dramatist to project the problems of a writer and intellectual of his own time and place onto the epoch of Hölderlin.

Therein, however, lies the difficulty for the reader or spectator. Weiss' figures, in *Hölderlin* as well as in the earlier play *Trotsky in Exile* (and in Weiss' monumental novel *The Aesthetics of Resistance* [1975–81]), are both identical and non-identical with their historical namesakes. The degree of fictionalization changes from work to work and from figure to figure—a complex and contradictory poetological method that the dramatist himself was never completely able to explain. The fictional Hölderlin in the play adheres to all the known facts about the historical Hölderlin. Nonetheless, on stage one is confronted with a character created by Peter Weiss and which he accurately summed up in these words: 'I wanted to describe something of the conflict that arises in a person who suffers to the point of madness from the injustices, the humiliations in his society, who completely supports the revolutionary upheavals, and yet does not find the praxis with which the misery can be remedied, who is ground down between his poetic vision and the reality of class separation, state power, military force.' This is a self-portrait of Weiss. At the same time it is a portrait of Hölderlin that coincides with the factual findings of Lukács, Bertaux, and others. The interpretation of Hölderlin's mental illness as an act of revolutionary resistance, however, remains Weiss' own. Here he parts ways with Bertaux who, in a later book, described Hölderlin's life after the onset of his illness as a petit-bourgeois idyll. In a lengthy notation in 1979 Weiss criticizes Bertaux's interpretation as trivializing and repeats his own hypothesis, which also constitutes the basis of his play—Hölderlin's condition was the consequence of his hypersensitive reaction to a 'hostile and sick environment'. The kind of illness, in other words, about which Weiss, after his *Trotsky* defeat, had noted: 'Our illnesses are mostly political illnesses.'

Easily overlooked in the play—as they are in real life—are the various brief appearances and comments by labourers, domestics, and gardeners. They are the foundation of society, as Weiss says in his Afterword to the play. Without their labour, it would not be possible for poets and philosophers—be they conformist or revolutionary—to spend their lives reflecting about different models of human coexistence. Without the working masses, the visions of a more just society remain just that.

This is the topic of the story of Empedocles, the play-within-the-play that Hölderlin performs for his friends in Homburg in 1799. Empedocles appears as a kind of messianic bearer of hope—a figure who recurs repeatedly in Weiss' work. Weiss uses the figure for the purpose of making the oppressed and exploited classes aware of their own strength and responsibility. Since the Agrigentians become all too dependent on Empedocles, the wise leader takes the ultimate step: he gives up his life for his people. A messiah whose sacrificial death is intended to make people not into objects of a heavenly power, but into subjects of history. This concept had already been at the center of Brecht's poem from the 1930s, '*Der Schuh des Empedokles*' (The Shoe of Empedocles), where, after Empedocles' disappearance, it is said about the Agrigentians, 'Still some of them postponed their questions until his [Empedócles'] return, while already others/tried to find the solution themselves.' The same thought is expressed by Weiss' Hölderlin, who suggests to a labourer the following meaning of his drama: 'Do not expect to be helped/if you fail to help yourselves.' These words were taken almost verbatim from the historical Hölderlin's first version of *Empedócles*: 'You cannot/be helped if you yourselves do not help yourselves.' This is the theme that underlies all of Weiss' work since *Marat/Sade*.

Robert Cohen, the author of Understanding Peter Weiss, *from which this introduction has been adapted by the author, is an adjunct professor of German at New York University. His study of Weiss' work was part of a series titled* Understanding Modern European and Latin American Literature, *published by the University of South Carolina Press. The excerpt is used by permission of the press.*

HÖLDERLIN

A PLAY IN TWO ACTS

CAST OF CHARACTERS

Hölderlin

Hegel

Schelling

Sinclair

Neuffer

Hiller

Schmid *

Ephorus Schnurrer (played by same actor as Autenrieth)

Professor Autenrieth*

Duke Karl Eugen

Hermokrátes*

Duchess Franziska

Charlotte von Kalb

Heinrich von Kalb

Fritz von Kalb

Henry Gontard

Christiane Zimmer

Lotte Zimmer

Wilhemene Kirms

Pánthea

Schiller

Goethe

Fichte

Susette Gontard

Jakob Gontard

Margarete Gontard

Gogel

Bethmann

Schellenberg

Pausánias

Glazier Wagner

Cabinet-Maker Zimmer

Buonarroti

Hölderlin's Mother

Editor of the *Rhenische Zeitung*

Male Workers

Female Workers

Students

Passers-by

Guests of the Gontards

Famuli

Attendant

An Officer

Gendarmes

Body Guards

Musicians

*Same actor plays both Hiller and Schmid; same actor plays both Ephorus Schnurrer and Professor Autenrieth; same actor plays Duke Karl Eugen and Hermokrátes; same actress plays Fritz von Kalb, Henry Gontard, Christiane Zimmer, and Lotte Zimmer; same actress plays Wilhelmine Kirms and Pánthea; same actor plays Glazier Wagner and Cabinet-Maker Zimmer; same actor plays Famulus and Attendant; same actor plays Gendarme and Bodyguard.

Act I

Prologue

The set is minimal. A couple of podiums and platforms can be used. Otherwise only those props that are absolutely essential for the play.

On stage, the students Hölderlin, Hegel, Hiller, Sinclair, and Schelling.

Sinclair, the youngest, a law student, wears knee breeches and open shirt. The others wear the uniform of the Theological Seminary: light black coat with white trim on cuffs and collar.

The clothing of the Singer is inconspicuous, hinting at his being a member of the peasantry. Same costume throughout the play.

All carry garlands and wreaths, with which they form a tableau around Hölderlin.

SINGER.
Prologue

HÖLDERLIN.
A play about the poet Hölderlin
cannot evade the darker aspects of this man
whose vision of a world restored
was mocked by history and by men ignored
True he saw the Bastille fall

and was as were so many others full
of praise of fraternity

ALL.
But the way to true justice and equality
soon proved longer than it once seemed to be

HÖLDERLIN.
Still in anno seventeen hundred ninety-three
in July in Tübingen at the Seminary
young scholars friends eagerly debate
the nature of democracy whose coming they await
They see the doors burst open wide
by France's revolutionary stride
yet though the light burst in like brilliant dawn
most Germans in their blindness slumber dumbly on

ALL.
For here though each man's cracked and broken life
is vexed oppressed consumed with strife
and envy each still meekly bends his knee
submissive to authority

HÖLDERLIN.
Not to bind himself to one particular
on earth to be at home no matter where
in language to fulfill his fate
to such ends he bent his will as best he might
but found his voice increasingly confined
by walls that closing in on him oppressed his mind
Relentless pressure kills the lucid thought,
stunts each day until the mind distraught
darkens For years he heard his words called mad by men
because their truth was beyond their ken.

The Group points at Hölderlin.

ALL.
And this continues into our own day
as long as such a one as he
confined within his tower has yet to be set free
and oppression is the rule and pain and poverty

HÖLDERLIN.
This play by definition is a tragedy
Yet spare me overmuch solemnity
for sorrow always must defer to joy
though I knew little of it in my day
Therefore bring music on whose company
shall banish tedium as each now has his say

The tableau dissolves.

SINGER.
When he first to the city came
the tower was already there
From the low window of his room
down he looked and saw it where
it rose beside the river
Strange it was that he should gaze
when first he to the city came
upon that prison of his later days

Scene 1

*Two comfortable armchairs. In the background, a wall. A
couple of posts on which to hang the decorations.*

*The Students hang the garlands and wreaths for a festive
occasion.*

Sinclair, carrying paint bucket and brush, paints on the wall:
LONG LIVE THE 14th OF JULY.

The following philosophical debate can take on a playful and ironic overtone if, meanwhile, the Students are busy hanging up the decorations.

SINGER.
First scene in which
Hölderlin and his student friends
debate the essence of freedom and
come into conflict with tyranny

Enter Neuffer: in traveling clothes and with a satchel.

SCHELLING.
How respectable and satisfied you look
Neuffer
You have moved well beyond this school
already smell of parson's fat

NEUFFER.
And you here in your oxen stall
are still bent mind and soul
on letting those famous pinions grow
that shall one day
lift you high above this stable dung
to dazzling deeds.

HEGEL.
You have plumped yourself down in the pulpit
and abandoned your longing for laurels
bestowed
by the muse's hand

Hölderlin approaches Neuffer.

HÖLDERLIN.
What choice have we but to groan
in the galleys of theology
or else to grow gaunt
under the yoke of pedagogy

He embraces Neuffer.

NEUFFER.
Holder
tell me thou block
and does the floor still creak to your wooden tread
as swept up in creative ecstasy
you search for rhymes and test the beat
by stomping the measures with your feet
and pacing the Augean stable
suddenly begin to mutter
bursts of confused words
knocking the roof beams with your head
swaying swooning swearing
then standing staring
out the garret window
at the steam rising
from the rushing River Styx

HÖLDERLIN.
I only wish that I too
could be as recklessly
jubilant as you are
so early in the morning
the worst of times
when day immensely fat
insurmountably puffed up
still lies before me

NEUFFER.
That's because it is madness
to try to fathom
what must for all time
lie beyond
our powers to comprehend

HEGEL.
Either you played the truant here or fell sound asleep
when we turned our backs on
the *Ding an sich*
that supreme essential which
defined by neither time nor space
consumed us all
from some unknown dimension
and kept us meekly cowed
And you had long since gone away
when we turned to other objects which
belonging to the visible world
permit investigation
of cause and effect.

NEUFFER.
In spite of which
you never shall come near
the source of knowledge

HEGEL.
Now that no such abstract
thing exists
and we have presented
the universe
with an I
a thinking I that is to say

the result is that the only true
reality
will henceforth be this I
which here and now
in this existence
thinks

HÖLDERLIN.
Once again our Hegel shows us how
we can orient ourselves by him
when bewildered we wonder where we stand
in relation to ourselves and to the world

HEGEL.
It is quite simple
Here
stands the subject man
there
his object which is the world.
Into the essence of this world
our mind penetrates
and through us the world
becomes pure knowing
Becoming thus of itself aware
the world in a never-ending process
creates itself in our mind

Neuffer shakes his head.

NEUFFER.
And where does that leave God

HEGEL.
God's kingdom will
on earth

come into being
democratically
And this kingdom
is not God-created
For us the divine is revealed
in man who
in the free republic of reason
attains the highest stage
of development
Do but consider how history
through all its contradictions and its tragedies
ascended step by step
as man became aware
that with his actions
he himself
shapes history

Hegel takes a pinch of snuff.

SINGER.
For society and all that it may contain
of property loss and monetary gain
of law of politics and family ties
of religion jurisprudence and morality
of all the haze of war- and state- and other craft
and of much-lauded science and whatever else is left
all these things that tradition consecrates
are part and parcel of what the mind creates

Hegel blows his nose.

NEUFFER.
I only know
that behind all things that we behold
a mysterious power is at work

SCHELLING.
And this same power it is
that compels us to
do what we do now
to wit
decorate this courtyard for
the visitation of
His Most Mighty and Most Gracious
Fatherly Excellency.

SINCLAIR.
Whom at the same time we repudiate.

SCHELLING.
A statement you will in turn repudiate
Sinclair
if they lock you up
So all remains as it was before

SINCLAIR.
No
Nothing remains as it was before.
The blade is sharpened
What we hang here now
are funeral wreaths

*Enter Ephorus Schnurrer, accompanied by two Famuli,
who carry cushions and a couple of footstools. Sinclair slips
away.*

SINGER.
Make way Make way
In splendid array,
the grand rector arrives
to take matters in hand

to defend the state
from mad plots
to assassinate potentates.

SCHNURRER.
Well well
Well done
Gentlemen allow me to
recall one matter to your mind
which is that in His Excellency's presence
you must not openly display
that liberal spirit which
prevails here at our school.
Rumors of democratic yes
even Jacobinic tendencies within this seminary
have reached the ducal ear
Master Hegel
once again you look a sight
Would you come before
His Excellency
as a genius in rags

HEGEL.
I overstep the limits
of my individuality and enter
the ordinary Which is to say
I'm working
which is why my clothes
are wearing out

SCHNURRER.
Go then in the corner there
and make yourself presentable
And what sort of unkempt coiffure

is this
Go now to Barber Hiller
and have him attend to it

*Hegel steps into the background, where he puts his rumpled
clothes in order. Hiller exits.*

SCHNURRER.
My dear Neuffer
How it pleases me
to see former seminarians
return for such festivities
I see in your return the proof
that something yet remains
of venerable tradition
of which these days
alas alas
all too easily
so much is lost

*He notices the slogans painted on the wall. For some
moments he stands speechless. Points at them.*

SCHELLING.
Menetekel Upharsin

*Sinclair returns, together with other Students. All gaze at
the text, astonished.*

SCHNURRER.
This is how
you would greet the Duke

SINCLAIR.
The man still staunchly supports
serfdom

SCHNURRER.
What sort of talk is this

SINCLAIR.
He supports the royalists
who sought and found refuge in Coblentz
and now when the Revolution
hangs by a single hair
he would mobilize
an army of the dispossessed within our land
to hurl against those French
who seek the restoration
of equality

SCHNURRER.
You will paint over those words
immediately.

A few Students exit.

SINCLAIR.
Did not you yourself
Ephorus Schnurrer
teach us Rousseau
and the Declaration
of the Rights of Man
drawn up across the Rhine

SCHNURRER.
To teach to be a scholar
of the turmoil of our time
is not at all the same
as to model one's behavior
anarchically after them
We shall investigate this matter

and make appropriate correction
Remember
each and every one of you
receives a stipend
from His Grace the duke.

Exit Schnurrer. The Students return with paint and
brushes. They paint over the slogans. The Famuli supervise
their work.

FAMULUS.
I told you it was foolish
to make a provocation
Without achieving anything
you risk your entire future

HÖLDERLIN.
O this whole scholar's life disgusts me
All this musty wisdom
that's force-fed into us
only clouds our eyes
to the essential
May all these bachelor
master doctor titles
be sent packing off to hell

SINGER.
How quick how quick
parents are to stick
the children of the pious poor
their souls broken with awe and fear
of God into this hole
where they are fed and where the goal
of all their training is that they
cleaned up and neatly dressed may

in this land of bunglers and barbarians
do what's expected of seminarians
defend hearth and home and native soil
Meanwhile these famuli play their role
To the students' asses they press their ears
and pass on what they hear to their superiors
It's totally absurd ridiculous

The Famulus steps menacingly closer.

HÖLDERLIN.
Yes Spy on
and by your spying earn
your pitiful livelihood
Denounce us do
so they may whip civility
into our very skin
O when I but think
of our ambitious parents
of how with detestable servility
they decked us out with imperial names
Johann Christian Friedrich Hölderlin
Friedrich Wilhelm Joseph Schelling
Georg Friedrich Wilhelm Hegel
I can only wonder
what they expected from us

*Hegel, in the meantime, has come downstage. Neuffer goes
over to him, sniffs.*

NEUFFER.
What have you been up to in the corner there
What's this I get a whiff of on your breath
O Hegel you'll drink up
what little reason you have left

*Neuffer takes a flask from Hegel's pocket, takes a swig,
hands the flask to Hölderlin, who drinks the last drops.*

FAMULUS.
I am duty bound
to report this incident

Hölderlin takes a pipe out of his pocket, starts to fill it.

HÖLDERLIN.
And report as well
that though we are forbidden to
we smoke
that though we are forbidden to
at night we steal out through the window
and drink ourselves unconscious
in the taverns of the town
Report it is a miracle
that we still breathe
when by rights we should have
long ago under this regimen
turned to stone

The Famulus tries to wrest the pipe from him.

HÖLDERLIN.
And furthermore
how dare this toady
even speak to us
Know your place
Remove your hat

*He knocks the Famulus' hat off. At the same moment,
Hiller runs in, his hair cut short. The Famulus exits, angry
and threatening.*

HILLER.
Comrades
the coaches draw near
that bear the despot
and here we stand
to welcome that plunderer
of men's labours
with our ovations

HEGEL.
Enough of that
Did we not
within our club
agree
to temper our opinions
and to proceed
for politic reasons
cautiously

HILLER.
That line has since been overstepped
The Revolution can no longer be
served by noble sentiments
You still hang back
quibbling in Arcadia
while in Paris
they are fighting for their lives

SCHELLING.
The Jacobins have brought
their present troubles on themselves
with their call for terror
Slicing off so many heads now
can only bring their own
beneath the blade

HILLER.
And if the feudal lords
had beat the Revolution down
and spread *their* reign of terror
what would have happened then
The Duke of Brunswick said
that he would level Paris
to the ground.

HEGEL.
Those who battled in the streets
still know themselves too little
are too self-estranged
to be able to establish
the true and proper state of liberation

SINCLAIR.
Progress
according to your theory
can only come about through strife
and conflict
The Revolution is
the most violent collision
and takes us
a giant stride forward

HEGEL.
Violence contains the element of revenge
of blindness and anxiety
What is toppled and crumbles
is but the surface
not the inner essence of this world
The ground of being
is the idea

When the idea
has taken hold of an entire age
then only is the time
for true renewal ripe
And the only way
to reach that end
is unceasing
patient
education

SINCLAIR.
For countless centuries
those in power have
crushed the weak
and when at last
they fought back
a humanistic wail went up
What gives these slaves
the right to think
they are entitled
to resort to violence

HEGEL.
The initial attempt must
in the violence of the movement
bring about its opposite
This is already happening
and what was rent
will mend itself again

SINCLAIR.
What happened in France
when everything seemed possible
that was impossible before

looms three hundred times
larger in our princely enclaves

HEGEL.
The Reformation
spared us from
the Revolution
We stand opposed
to absolute freedom
because
it leads to the decline
and death
of individual values
For us
the principle holds true
that what ought to happen
must happen
only through insight
and reflection

SINCLAIR.
Death to all tyrants

HEGEL.
The informers hear you
A wretched revolutionary he
who dreams he's always standing
at a barricade

Sinclair runs to the upstage wall. He writes in large letters:
LONG LIVE THE REVOLUTION.

SINGER.
So we see how the mind freed from one school of
    thought

constructs its own to compensate
Yet when these thinkers try to predict or foretell
their thoughts mostly stay inside their own skull
The thinkers think but don't get embroiled
Nor has all their knowledge enlightened the world
Meanwhile those whose labor supports society
are never asked but would have plenty to say

*From one side the vanguard of the Duke's escort appears:
drummers, trumpeter, and standard bearers. One of the
standards bears the Württemberg coat of arms, with the
inscription: FEARLESS AND TRUE.*

Drum roll.

*From the other side a couple of Farm Workers—two men
and a woman—enter.*

*Behind the vanguard, escorted by Bodyguards, appear the
Duke and Duchess, in full regalia.*

*They are followed by a bemedalled Ephorus Schnurrer and
by Teachers, Famuli, and Students.*

The ducal couple are escorted to their places of honour.

FIRST MALE WORKER.
And to him we must hand over our sons
so they can die for five kreutzers
on the banks of the Schelde and the Rhine
so he can go on strutting and rutting
far from the smoke and din of the battle line

FEMALE WORKER.
Our hut's too small for the family
while this one here lives in luxury
at Grafeneck Einsiedel Hohnheim
Wants us to build a new moated castle even more splendid

because he's got so much gold he's at a loss how to
   spend it

SECOND MALE WORKER.
One day we will rise up too
and there'll be an end to this ducal hullabaloo
with drum roll and trumpet and all the rest
because we will grind this fellow into the dust

A flourish of trumpets. The Students line up in rows.
Ephorus, Teachers, and Famuli remain standing behind
the ducal pair. Cushions are pushed behind the backs of
their Majesties, their feet placed on footstools.

Sinclair, unobserved, has completed writing the text and
joined his friends.

The Workers exit.

SCHNURRER AND CHORUS OF TEACHERS.
Our most humble wish is now fulfilled
and this fine summer day with joy instilled
for Eugen Duke of Württemberg and Tek is come
together with his spouse Franziska for one sole end and
   aim
by graciously inspecting himself to reassure
that this seminary's fame unsullied by rumours remains
   secure.

CHORUS OF STUDENTS.
To celebrate this hour may we
with all due reverence and propriety
sum up our heart-felt veneration by
raising a cheer as with one voice we cry
Long live our honoured guests

SCHNURRER.
Long may they live

ALL.
Hurrah Hurrah Hurrah

SINCLAIR.
Long live the twelve thousand
Württemberger troops
sold by the duke
to the Netherlands

General commotion

SCHNURRER.
Bring the troublemaker here

HÖLDERLIN.
It was I

Schelling claps a hand over Hölderlin's mouth.

SHOUTS.
It was Sinclair

SCHNURRER.
What
Isaac von Sinclair
a nobleman and still
so young
and what's more a student of the law.

FAMULUS.
And he painted that
on the wall too

He points to the slogan painted on the wall. The Duke has risen. A couple of Famuli rush downstage and seize Sinclair.

THE DUKE.
Did you paint that
on the wall

SINCLAIR.
Yes

HÖLDERLIN.
We all did

Schelling tries to calm Hölderlin.

SCHNURRER.
This only proves
alas alas
how contagious is
this freedom-fraud
that spreads from France.
And since your Ducal Excellence
highly prizes order
authority and strict adherence to the law
as clear warning and example
to all others
this boy shall now
in public
undergo the bastinado

The Famuli have dragged Sinclair downstage. A Famulus swings him up over his shoulder. Another Famulus pulls down his trousers. The Famulus who is carrying Sinclair bends forward, exhibiting Sinclair's bare buttocks to the distinguished company. Hölderlin screams.

HÖLDERLIN.
No
Not this
Basta basta

Schelling embraces Hölderlin, holds him tight.

SCHNURRER.
And following these proceedings
Stipendiary Hölderlin shall
for his impertinence
be confined to the cell for six hours

*The Duke has sat down again. The Duchess, however, rises
to view the proceedings at close range through her lorgnette.*

SCHNURRER.
The rod

A rod is handed to him.

SCHNURRER.
Have you founded
a secret society

Sinclair does not answer. Schurrer beats him.

A collective gasp.

SCHNURRER.
Have you founded
a secret society

SINCLAIR.
Yes

SCHNURRER.
What is its name?

Sinclair does not reply. Schnurrer beats him. A gasp.

SINCLAIR.
The Harmonists

SCHNURRER.
Who are the members
of this society

Sinclair remains silent.

HÖLDERLIN.
Johann Christian Friedrich Hölderlin

HILLER.
Christian Friedrich Hiller

SCHNURRER.
Who else

SHOUTS.
Hegel
Schelling

SCHNURRER.
Do you sanction
regicide

Sinclair does not reply. Schnurrer beats him.

HEGEL.
We do not sanction
regicide

Sinclair starts to sing as Schnurrer continues to beat him.

SINCLAIR.
Tremble ye tyrants tremble

The day of vengeance nighs
Grim shall be the tyrant's downfall
when the oppressed arise

Hölderlin collapses, starts to sob. Schelling and Neuffer try to comfort him.

THE DUKE.
I trust you also sing
that charming ditty
scribbled by
the rabble of Marseilles

A SHOUT.
Schelling translated it

THE DUKE.
Is that so
Master Schelling

SCHELLING.
Excellency
we all have our failings

Meanwhile, Sinclair continues to sing as Schnurrer beats him.

SINCLAIR.
Allons enfants de la patrie.

The Duke rises and, with a wave of his hand, concludes the punishment. He puts an arm around the shoulders of the panting and puffing Ephorus and leads him back to his chair. Two Famuli carry Sinclair behind the row of Students.

Friends help the sobbing Hölderlin up.

THE DUKE.
Since that today we find ourselves inclined
to be merry merciful and of a lenient mind
we shall distract ourself no longer here
nor yet sever our attachment to so dear
a place to us as this
whose worthy educative mission is
to train new pastors and new teachers who
on setting forth shall devote their lives unto
conscientious service whose end shall be
to serve both state and Christianity

The Dignitaries applaud.

THE DUKE.
We are assured
that your careers can be pursued
in swift-ensuing peace
for even now we have received from Coblenz
news from France
which now spreads like wildfire
throughout free Europe
That most monstrous and most steeped-in-blood
of all the Jacobins
the red Marat
has
by an aristocratic heroine
been stabbed to death

A few seconds of silence. Then screams, weeping.

SHOUTS.
The Revolution lives on
Down with the nobility
Dispossess the rich

All power to the workers
Long live democracy
Vive la Liberté

*The Bodyguards and the Famuli push back the Students.
Then departure of the ducal pair and their retinue
becomes an impressive demonstration of power. The rebellious Students stand expectantly in the background. When
the Procession, escorted by the Guard, has gone, Hiller
leaps forward, unfurls a French tricolour. Another Student
rips the Württhemberg banner from its pole. The tricolor is
wrapped around the pole, which is hung with garlands
and wreaths and held high. Hiller, Schelling, Neuffer, and
some other Students gather around this symbol of freedom.
Hölderlin goes to Sinclair and leads him downstage toward
the group.*

Only Hegel stands off to one side.

HILLER.
He who would help men be free
through revolution
can rest nowhere
or only in his grave.

Hegel has taken a pinch of snuff; he sneezes.

Scene 2

*A couple of chairs. A chaiselongue. A table with wine carafe
and glasses. A bed. An embroidery frame. A harpsichord.*

*In the background, guns hung one above the other. On a stand,
a large coat, hat, and game bag. At the harpsichord, Charlotte
von Kalb. Hölderlin accompanies her on the flute.*

Major Heinrich von Kalb in an armchair, his legs outstretched.

Charlotte's companion, Wilhelmine Kirms, at the embroidery frame.

Fritz von Kalb (played by an actress) is lying on the floor.

SINGER.
Second scene in which
Hölderlin puts to use
his erudition
in order to discover
what sort of living
he can make from it

He introduces those present on stage, while Charlotte and Hölderlin continue playing the sonata.

The son of the house Fritz von Kalb
lying on the floor eleven years old
Wilhelmene Kirms well-educated
lady's companion yet emancipated
could be much more useful sits instead
prettily stitching embroidery thread
Frau Charlotte accompanying Hölderlin's triller
is famed for being close to Schiller
It was on Schiller's recommendation
that Hölderlin took up his present station
Major Heinrich von Kalb sprawled out here
for the charms of music has no ear
would rather take part in wars and invasions
killing the foe and planting flags in foreign nations.
The scene is Waltershausen fall of the year
seventeen hundred ninety-four

Hölderlin suddenly stops playing. Charlotte plays a few more bars, but now bungling the notes. The Major claps, bored. Fritz von Kalb crawls around. Hölderlin slips his flute into its case. Frau von Kalb steps away from the harpsichord, sits down next to her Companion. The Singer closes the harpsichord. The Companion pours a glass of wine for Frau von Kalb. Fritz von Kalb now on his knees in front of his father.

FRITZ VON KALB.
Sir now tell me
how you sailed
with your frigate
to New Orleans

HEINRICH VON KALB.
The day our frigate docked
in the harbour of New Orleans
a slave ship
had just arrived
from Africa

FRITZ VON KALB.
How many slaves were in the hold

HEINRICH VON KALB.
At least a thousand naked slaves
lay stacked in rows from keel
to deck from stem to stern.
Each two chained
hand to hand and foot to foot

FRITZ VON KALB.
And were there children and women
and new-born babies too

and was there stench and screaming
and did the dead lie in between

*The Major lifts Fritz onto his knees. Hölderlin has seated
himself on a chair. He picks up a book, leafs through it,
then simply sits, weary and distracted.*

HEINRICH VON KALB.
The buyers already crowd the quay
The hammer falls The bidding starts again
as now the husband from his wife is torn
the child from its mother's arms

FRITZ VON KALB.
And they have come into a land
where so they say all men are free
created equal and born with a right
to life and liberty

HEINRICH VON KALB.
Even so my son
So it is written
in the Declaration of Independence
for which I fought body and soul
under my General Lafayette.

FRITZ VON KALB.
And why does it not apply to those
whose skin is black
or copper-coloured

HEINRICH VON KALB.
There is you see this difference
in colour
Dark races are by nature
base and they moreover lack

all education
The white man on the other hand
is well endowed with every gift
and he is called upon to spread
that highest of all goods
his culture
wheresoever he may venture
in this world

FRITZ VON KALB.
And why then
does he keep slaves

HEINRICH VON KALB.
Face to face
with President Washington
I understood his view
to be that while slavery
ill accords with the enlightened mind
many generations
of strict discipline
will be required before
the blackamoor learns
to comport himself in society

FRITZ VON KALB.
And why then does
the white man gun down
the Huron and
the Iroquois

HEINRICH VON KALB.
In North America
the settler's life is difficult
Before ideals can be implanted there

the settler first must fight to survive
for the people living in those woods
are wild as animals
relieve themselves
casually and anywhere
rend the white man's flesh
with their bare teeth

FRITZ VON KALB.
But the land is theirs
They must defend themselves
against the invaders

The Major shoves Fritz off his lap.

HEINRICH VON KALB.
I trust your tutor
taught you that

*Hölderlin sits up. He takes his pipe from his jacket pocket,
starts to fill it.*

HEINRICH VON KALB.
You will not smoke this room up with that pipe

Hölderlin puts his pipe back into his pocket.

HÖLDERLIN.
Major I have tried to explain to your son
a little of the early history
of that land in which the peaceful nations
of the Indians
flourished up to the day
they found themselves confronted with
what we call civilization

HEINRICH VON KALB.

Of far more worth than
their tromping around in circles
and clicking their tongues
is our store of knowledge
which we patiently seek
to impart to these
unformed creatures

HÖLDERLIN.

Yet if you will permit me Major
they live in harmony with nature.
The language of the plants
as of the sky
to them reveals its meaning
and in any wilderness
they find their way
read significant signs
in all that lives
which we despite our senses
are blind to.

HEINRICH VON KALB.

That sounds to me
like poeticizing

HÖLDERLIN.

If I may
it is not only in the realm of poetry
that harmony must be restored
between nature and mankind
but just now in France
the attempt was undertaken
with the establishment of the cult

of nature as the supreme being
to unite the country
in a new state religion

HEINRICH VON KALB.
Bravo Bravo
And meanwhile your incorruptible
and virtuous Robespierre
started lopping heads

CHARLOTTE VON KALB.
O enough of these atrocities

HEINRICH VON KALB.
It served him right
that they smashed his jaw
and then lopped his own head
from his body

CHARLOTTE VON KALB.
No more of this

FRITZ VON KALB.
They held it up high then dropped it in a basket
and sang the *Marseillaise*
which is now forbidden.

Hölderlin claps his hands over his face.

HEINRICH VON KALB.
Nature is raw and unruly
When man withdraws his civilizing hand
it runs riot

*Fritz von Kalb stands as if preparing to deliver a formal
recitation. He speaks in an innocent voice.*

FRITZ VON KALB.

As they teach the rude redskins good manners with guns
and use whips to teach blacks how to toil in all seasons
so the son and heir of the worthy major
is hounded from ignorance like a beast from its lair
and like a savage waits to be wakened from deepest night
by civilization's dawning light

*Charlotte von Kalb and Wilhelmine Kirms try to take the
poem lightly. They hope that their laughter will keep the
Major from losing his temper.*

HEINRICH VON KALB.

What sort of dangerous
and mind-bewildering utterance is this
You give this boy
too free a rein Doctor

*Hölderlin passes his hands over his face and head. Fritz
von Kalb continues with feigned innocence.*

FRITZ VON KALB.

And my duty is to thank you sir
and also kiss your paternal hand
when you have punished as the black man me
or as the red-skinned Indian

Major von Kalb leaps up. Hölderlin retreats into himself.

HEINRICH VON KALB.

Listen my son
We are destined to subdue
and dominate this world
Thus for you a different regimen obtains
than what's appropriate
for primitives

skulking in dark continents
In you it seeks its purpose
to prepare the chosen
the superior man
to manage his possessions
and profit by doing so

CHARLOTTE VON KALB.
Heinrich don't excite yourself
Our Herr Hölderlin is doing all
that lies within his power
to purge our son of his wilfulness
and his beneficent influence
has helped our boy greatly
even in the one year
he has spent here
in our midst

*The Major stomps off into the background, searches for his
coat. The Singer helps him into his coat, hands him his
game bag and flintlock.*

CHARLOTTE VON KALB.
What is it then Heinrich
So late and you would
still go out

HEINRICH VON KALB.
To hunt

The Major shoulders his gun.

FRITZ VON KALB.
To shoot the hind
between her eyes

Major von Kalb exits, accompanied by the Singer.

Hölderlin takes out his pipe but remains seated, awaiting permission to light his pipe. Wilhelmine Kirms fills Charlotte's wine glass. Charlotte von Kalb starts to sob convulsively and hysterically.

FRITZ VON KALB.
When father's away
mama cries differently
than when he is with her there
in the room

Charlotte drinks up, pours herself another glass.

CHARLOTTE VON KALB.
Go my boy and
dress yourself for night
and also wash yourself
from head to foot
with cold water as
the doctor told you to

Exit Fritz von Kalb.

CHARLOTTE VON KALB.
You may feel free to smoke now
Holder.

Hölderlin lights his pipe, picks up his book again.

CHARLOTTE VON KALB.
How fine it feels
to be alone
with kindred spirits
O what a burden life imposes on us
with this institution

marriage
which we enter into
with little inclination
You dear Wilhelmine
escaped this prison
just in time

WILHELMINE KIRMS.
Not once but twice
a woman must revolt
not only against
the injustice suffered
at the ruler's hand
by the oppressed
but against as well
that tyranny entrenched
in the so-called bosom
of the family

CHARLOTTE VON KALB.
In Paris
the women did their share

WILHELMINE KIRMS.
Yes they were good enough to carry muskets
and ammunition
to bind the warrior's wounds
and dig their graves
They baked the bread and stirred the soup
and stormed the Tuileries
but what did the revolutionary mouth say then
Back to the mattress woman
That's where you belong

CHARLOTTE VON KALB.

My poor Heinrich considers
himself completely in the right
and fully grasps
the guiding principles
of the American and French
Revolutions.

WILHELMINE KIRMS.
Yes Man makes great proclamations of justice
throughout the world
and is pleased to take possession
of his wife's house and money and body
and swells with pride when he takes over
her land with crops and livestock
as if it had been his
since time began

CHARLOTTE VON KALB.
You must not use such language
dearest friend

WILHELMINE KIRMS.
Feeble feeble
is that entire sex
together with what dangles
between their legs

CHARLOTTE VON KALB.
Shh Wilhelmene Shh
The boy can hear
The evil his body plagues him with
is trouble enough

HÖLDERLIN.
Most gracious Frau Charlotte

CHARLOTTE VON KALB.
Not most gracious
Holder
How often must I tell you
that you must see in me a friend
who out of tenderheartedness
is drawn to you

HÖLDERLIN.
Frau Charlotte
I can no longer
help you with your son
The long nights spent
sleepless at his bedside
have destroyed me
I have tried mildness
Force had been applied in excess
by the worthy major
Yet when on rare occasion
I think his restlessness
has calmed at last
and tiptoe to his bed
still I find him in convulsions
at his vice

CHARLOTTE VON KALB.
And here we placed our confidence
in your ability
as a student of theology and the humanities
to find the means
to heal his derangement

HÖLDERLIN.
I have always acquainted him with
worthy objects

have understood my duty as his tutor
to preserve in him
so long as possible
the original state
of innocence and purity
I read him Homer
poems
created under the open sky
themselves outgrowths of nature
I hold before him lofty
ideal figures
Pindar Heraclitus
Plutarch
and he all he ever says is
Why are the Jacobins
now called the rabble
Why was the red priest
Jacques Roux
forced to stab himself to death
Why
was Buonarroti
thrown into prison
Why
does Saturn
eat his own children
Who is
Leviathan

He beats his head with his fists.

CHARLOTTE VON KALB.
In what distress o
in what distress
we find ourselves

How should the child's mind
be healed
when we are ringed about
with arson murder rape
and do not know
if soon the air will shake
with cannon
I see my own life passing by
and nothing
gives me courage

*Charlotte von Kalb rises with difficulty. Begins to sob
again. Suddenly, passionately embraces Hölderlin.*

HÖLDERLIN.
But dearest dearest

CHARLOTTE VON KALB.
If only I had someone close to me
as young as you are
and as beautiful

She embraces him again, then breaks away.

CHARLOTTE VON KALB.
Come to me Wilhelmine
to my room
I find it too sad
to be alone

*She walks unsteadily, groping her way as if blind. After
she exits, Wilhelmine Kirms pours a glass of wine for
Hölderlin, holds it out to him, but he does not take it;
paces up and down.*

*As he paces, Hölderlin begins to mumble rhythmically,
then gradually forms words.*

HÖLDERLIN.

I must leave this house I cannot stay
Here one can no longer comprehend
thoughts that crowd upon the mind
All here must wither away
No image can now be created
the horizon blocked and barricaded
Yet the poem must it not stand free
rise above to see the whole of time
not just the sickly day
Should show man that the world is his
and how within it to fulfil his promise

WILHELMINE KIRMS.

When you talk so Hölderlin
it seems to me
as if I hear you calling back
from far away
or as if it would only be heard
by those who will come later.

Hölderlin stomps on.

HÖLDERLIN.

Nothing for us is lost or gone
but we can get back to it again
wherever we may be
What once in ages past was spoken
flows around us like the wind
We feel and hear the voices clear
They live within our senses
and renew themselves within
Though none may hear me now
later one will come
in whom I will begin again

WILHELMINE KIRMS.
You think of posterity
but fail to see
what is in front of your eyes

Hölderlin looks at her in bewilderment, as if he had for-
gotten that she was there.

WILHELMINE KIRMS.
In this house
in stable farm and village
in church and marketplace
and when the recruiting officer
comes to take the boys
and the tax collector calls
and when the maid
strangles her child
and up in the hayloft
the farmhand bellows
in his impotence
there you have the world
bursting to the fill
and have no need
to look about for
your pictures

Hölderlin hides his face in his hands.

WILHELMINE KIRMS.
Yes Do Shut out
the outside world
and devote yourself
to the inward gaze

Hölderlin turns away. Wilhelmine Kirms rises. She opens
the top of her dress.

WILHELMINE KIRMS.
For instance here
close at hand:
is my skin.

*Holding her dress wide open, she stands, challenging him
to touch her. Hölderlin freezes.*

WILHELMINE KIRMS.
Come Touch me

Hölderlin shrinks from her. Kirms laughs.

WILHELMINE KIRMS.
Does it frighten you so
if a woman
of her own free will
and for pleasure only
not because she is obliged to
seeks out a man

Hölderlin looks at her, completely bewildered.

WILHELMINE KIRMS.
Submissive soft
undemanding
yielding
that's what he wants
of a woman
so that she will not take away the ground
from under his feet

Hölderlin stammers.

HÖLDERLIN.
This wallowing throng
is hideous

the way the world
with all its bodies writhes
and sticks and smacks its lips
in sweat
and groans in darkness as
mindlessly
it breeds

Wilhelmine Kirms walks, laughing, past Hölderlin.

WILHELMINE KIRMS.
If you won't
attend to me
then I'll attend to
our lady

*Wilhelmine Krims exits. Immediately thereafter, Fritz von
Kalb appears in his nightshirt.*

FRITZ VON KALB.
I heard everything

*Hölderlin makes as if to strike Fritz, then restrains himself
and points to the chaiselongue. Fritz lies down there, pulls
the sheet up over himself. Hölderlin picks up his book
again, sits on a chair close to the bed.*

Fritz sits up.

FRITZ VON KALB.
Holder
they're hammering
and banging
out in the barn

HÖLDERLIN.
What do you mean

FRITZ VON KALB.
Hansel's doing it
with Gretel

HÖLDERLIN.
Where did you learn such language

FRITZ VON KALB.
In the kitchen

HÖLDERLIN.
When I assumed
my post as tutor
I did so out of my respect
for your mother and
to make good my promise
to both her and Herr von Schiller
to initiate you into
the humanities

FRITZ VON KALB.
All mama wants to do
is play the coquette
What I know about Greek
she wishes she could learn
in French

*Hölderlin bounds up, resumes his stomping. Hisses and
mutters rhythmically. Stops for long moments. Listens as if
caught up in hallucinations. Fritz von Kalb observes him
anxiously, sitting bolt upright.*

Hölderlin's sounds gradually take shape as words.

HÖLDERLIN.
It stuns the mind to hear
how they mock and jeer

all that language means to us:
the best impulse deep within
that makes us feel at one
in every sense harmonious
yet is so frail
so easily corruptible
that a single sound
serves to confound
its clarity Nor can one ever bring
language to both mean and sing
unless constant constant constant practice
set it free

Fritz von Kalb screaming in terror, while Hölderlin continues snorting and pacing.

FRITZ VON KALB.
Your blather makes me fart
I shit on all your art
Give me a woman's slit
I would rather stare at it
than hear you rant and watch you drool
Beat me now you stupid fool

Fritz beats himself. Then crawls down under the blanket.

HÖLDERLIN.
Into our language already an evil drone
has stolen of lies and of derision
Dreadful orders shrill
compel each man to kneel
and all protection lost obey
Our words confused lose their way
clank on like automatons
the voices blind and dumb

Easy prey and soon to carrion reduced
And your speech lies sprawled in rubble dust

Hölderlin, breathing heavily, remains near the bed. Then goes on in a muted voice.

HÖLDERLIN.
This is the peril that before us lies
that we shall hideously disguise
ourselves in total silence
The images we live by freeze
withdraw condemn us
to a living death We are so close
a single step will sunder us
from all we know No names Just babble
Nothing to hold on to to prevent the fall
And what lies ahead is bottomless

He stands listening. Then bends over the bed. Pulls back the blanket.

HÖLDERLIN.
What are you doing Fritz
You will destroy yourself.

Mindlessly and sobbing, he beats Fritz. Fritz screams. Hölderlin sinks to his knees in front of him. Passing by, the Singer, with two Farmworkers.

SINGER.
It's a big house with four towers
Can withstand big storms and lashing showers
but thick walls are no protection
against fear despair and desperation

FIRST FARMWORKER.

Among the upper classes fretting is a habit
We don't have time for it

SINGER.

That one however amid failure and misfortune
still seeks to expand his view to find within
what is vanishing and what will soon be gone
his way toward the image of a new man

SECOND FARMWORKER.

We weren't cut out for that sort of thing
What we'll hand down is a few songs to sing
in the streets and marketplace in the town
While these folks wallow in their world-pain and woe
we have fieldwork to do and out we go
to harvest the hay in summer and fall
and build rooms for them so they can dwell
undisturbed while they study their navel

Scene 3

In the background, a lectern at which Goethe stands, reading
through the pages of a manuscript.

SINGER.

Third scene in which
Hölderlin dares
to present himself
without reservation
as a poet
submitting himself
to the judgement

of the truly great
The setting is Jena the time of year
third of November of 'ninety-four

Schiller enters with Hölderlin. Schiller's hand on
Hölderlin's shoulder. Hölderlin very agitated.

HÖLDERLIN.
No I do not speak of a return
to the world of ancient Greece but rather
of the need to find
symbols
for our time
that are
as were the gods and myths of old
effective and able to sustain us

SCHILLER.
In antiquity man's actions
were part of a harmonious whole
The ideal and
the real were one and the same
But today the ideal and the real
have split
and the real
and the harmony of man's being
can be found if at all
in the idea

HÖLDERLIN.
The French revolutionaries too
chose Greek art
to represent the coming clarity
and greatness

SCHILLER.
Until now
all efforts
to find a just
form of government
have shattered
on the lack
of maturity within the individual
To achieve renewal
you must first create
a fully developed
character
through aesthetic schooling
Made spiritually destitute by mercantilism
deafened and torn
by the machinery of wheels
chained to fragments
a mere fragment himself
this is man

HÖLDERLIN.
Yet I just learned from you
that art can serve as a weapon
in the battle to establish
a dignified existence
Were I to allow
the contradiction between
the high poetical calling
and society's
backwardness to thwart me
my mission as poet
would be doomed

SCHILLER.

The time of pure unmediated creation
is past
In the dreadful empire
of objectification
little islands only
have remained for us
where our seeds
for a gradual transformation
can germinate

*Hölderlin jerks free of Schiller's paternal embrace. He pas-
sionately tries to persuade Schiller.*

HÖLDERLIN.

All forms and ways of thinking
must be shaken up and
overthrown totally
We are taking part
in the last and greatest
work of man
Never again the scornful look
never again the trembling of the people
in the presence of the sages and the priests
All for each and
each for all
Writing we see
the dawn
of a new age

SCHILLER.
Yet you must
observe the meter
Constantly you make us

stumble
over your metrics
Your leaping
and uncertain syntax
confuses us
True art
fulfills its meaning
only when it rouses one
to defend the beautiful
In the beautiful
our dissonances
are reconciled
Beauty is
freedom incorporate
Therefore beauty
goes before
freedom

In the course of their walk, they have approached Goethe.
Schiller introduces Hölderlin.

SCHILLER.
This honored master
is the young Hölderlin
a couple of whose efforts
I gave you for perusal
Would like to pursue
his studies here in Jena
since things did not work out for him
at Waltershausen
with our von Kalbs

Hölderlin makes a deep bow to Goethe without, however,
understanding who it is he has just met. He also hasn't

been listening because he goes right on with his conversa-
tion with Schiller. He immediately resumes pacing.

HÖLDERLIN.
We must turn our back on
what is at hand
yes renounce it
and pierce through
the sluggishness of what is now
and on the other side
of all that is familiar
find the extraordinary

SCHILLER.
You should not be
so presumptuous
You seek to cast
a new fantastic light
on the old landscapes
I understand that
But instead of hymns
upon the presentiments of a dream
we would prefer
the image of that reality
which encompasses this dream

HÖLDERLIN.
You do not see
how all things
are related to each other
see only particular details
in what is for me
the unity
within diversity

I envisage a larger frame
that reconciles contraries
Poems are for me
gigantic boulders of
the richest and most luminous
matter

SCHILLER.
Flee
from the philosophic matters
on which the best minds
destroy themselves
with fruitless wrestling
Stay closer
to the world of the senses
and you will be less in danger
of losing sobriety
and of falling prey to artificiality
I would also warn you
against the original sin
of German poets
namely the loose rambling style
that in an endless flood of verses
stifles the happiest thoughts

Hölderlin shows signs of exhaustion.

HÖLDERLIN.
I admit Herr von Schiller,
that I battle
with your genius
and that my fear
of being wholly ruled by you
hinders the clarity of my expression

Confronted with
what you and Herr von Goethe
have wrought to such perfection
I can only stammer

Goethe looks up. He studies Hölderlin for a few moments.

GOETHE.
Even Goethe would advise
that one who senses in himself
the inclination toward poetry
should not too quickly strive
to the higher reaches of art
where he would hardly know
how to find his way
Goethe might much rather wish
that the poet had first devoted himself
to the active life or science
so that after following a broad path
he might grow certain of his talent

Hölderlin is annoyed by this interruption. Turns to Schiller.

HÖLDERLIN.
I cannot surpass
your classic Greek
ideal of beauty
I know you are repelled
when I include within my world
its ceaseless disintegration
when I set out from its flux
and flow
and search for signs to show
how all boundaries break down
how the kingdom of the dead

mingles with our very breath
and heathen cults
oracular utterances remote adventures
are threaded through our thoughts

Goethe lifts up the sheaf of manuscript poems.

GOETHE.
I have carefully perused
your ejaculations
in which the naive is repeatedly juxtaposed
with accomplished formulae
Your writings do indeed bear the stamp
of both the crisis and the nervous agitation
with which our days are filled
But the question now arises
what aim had you in mind
You clarify nothing
You only add
to the rank growth
of the monstrous
which from all sides
closes in around us

Hölderlin brusquely turns to Schiller. With strong strides,
pulls him away from Goethe.

HÖLDERLIN.
I see it thus
There is
surrounding us
a nameless toiling
a labouring that longs
at last to cast
that which smothers it like clay

chokes off every view
stifles every cry for help
to a blind groan
To fight one's way out from under
to scrape off the mould
to find the hand
reaching up beside you
and then
to clear a way
for this
one needs
a universal
language

GOETHE.
First it takes
an equable temperament
then an eye that
perceives objects clearly
a mind that loves
what it beholds and finally
the urge of the hand
to recreate
what is seen
You might then
select a simple idyllic subject
and draw it for us
with modesty
We should be pleased to see
how well you fare
with the portraiture of man
on which in the end so much depends

HÖLDERLIN.

There is no place for modesty
or satisfaction
until the tremendous outcry
for the upheaval of society
compels us to listen
The question we must answer is
how the writer
in his whole being
stands in relation to his time

He pivots, turns to Schiller.

HÖLDERLIN.

You yourself Herr Schiller
placed your hope in the Revolution
were made an honorary citizen
of France

SCHILLER.

The leaders there
were unable to control
the fury of the lower
and more populous classes
and so when the great hour struck
it needs must
be wasted in the unleashing
of brute impulses

HÖLDERLIN.

It is not the poor and hungry
who are to blame for the excesses
It is the upper classes who
in France and throughout Europe

will not relinquish
their lust to dominate

SCHILLER.
Let us bend our efforts
to the creation of
a new morality
Let us beware
of any rashness
that impedes the common good
The task of achieving freedom
is one that requires
more than
a century

Hölderlin strikes his forehead with the palm of his hand.

SINGER.
Yes strike your forehead rack your brain
How can you ever hope to attain
a goal that none has yet reached in poetry
How through brilliant thoughts show the way
to what can be done on earth and in our day

Yes tug your hair and break your skull
How can you compel the ideal
to come down to earth and how transmute
the noble forms conceived by thought
into a physical force that can regenerate

SCHILLER.
Before the structures of society
can be changed
man himself
must be changed

HÖLDERLIN.
No
First all
from the ground up
must be overthrown
before the new
can come to be

Goethe, meanwhile, has put together and set aside the manuscript.

GOETHE.
We find much turmoil and rebellion
in the authors of our day
but common mortals do not understand
their calls to action
The revolutionaries are full of complaints
and each blames the other
for his own misfortune
Will-o'-the-wisps in the colourful fog
they lack the skill to build the bridge
between art and life
Their speech is full of the universal
yet nowhere can they find a sense of belonging
Only when they give up
their egoism and
embrace the values
shared by all men
will they be saved

HÖLDERLIN.
The blush of shame
shall one day
make his face red

who still today
chooses to remain
within the ice-cold zone
of the prevailing order

Goethe prepares to go. He turns to Schiller.

GOETHE.
I will stroll awhile in your garden then
and look forward to our discussion
of the form and content of our journal
There's much in the submitted manuscripts
that remains to be carefully reviewed
because I deem it unsuitable
to the society of worthy friends
This very hour I was once again reminded
of my concern that for the sake of the common good
it is best to set aside political interests
and that our magazine should treat only
what is purely human and above
all contemporary influence

Goethe exits.

HÖLDERLIN.
Who was that man then
who kept us from
this conversation that
I so looked forward to

SCHILLER.
What
Did you not recognize
the privy counselor

HÖLDERLIN.
What sort of privy
counselor

SCHILLER.
Herr von Goethe.

HÖLDERLIN.
Goethe

He opens his mouth wide to scream.

SINGER.
And donkey-like he dropped his jaw
and brayed aloud Hee haw Hee haw

Hölderlin brays.

HÖLDERLIN.
Hee haw
Hee haw

Scene 4

A lectern on a platform. A huge blackboard.

Assembled Students and young Academicians, among them Hölderlin, Schelling, Sinclair, and Siegfried Schmid (played by the actor who plays Hiller).

The Singer accompanied by four Farm Workers, two male, two female.

FIRST MALE WORKER.
The Herr von Goethe as Privy Counselor
has his hands full as administrator

at Ilmenau We work in the silver mines there
When tunnels cave in he'll oversee the repair

FIRST FEMALE WORKER.
He's also the senior management officer
in Apolda in charge of the manufacture
of stockings and bodices that our daughters knit
providing the income for the duke and his court

SECOND MALE WORKER.
But he opposed conscription and shared his view
with the duke Opposed the coalition of princes too
I know about this from a neighbour
who read it in the newspaper

SECOND FEMALE WORKER.
And Schiller they say is writing theatre pieces
attacking landlords and their accomplices
That takes courage these days His health isn't good
He suffers from seizures and spits blood

FIRST MALE WORKER.
But theatre isn't for the unwashed classes
It's for fancy dressers who have opera glasses
and manicured hands We can't attend
What they call Art has rules we don't understand

FIRST FEMALE WORKER.
In Weimar they're building another elegant theatre
which they keep picking our pockets to pay for
Then taking their cue from Goethe they repeat one
    and all
true culture comes only from the depths of the people

SECOND MALE WORKER.
They say there's a professor in the university who
talks about revolution to students a well-read crew
The question is does this cultured lot
know what to do with what they're taught
Most have had their fill of France and all it stands for
Revolution should stay on the other side of the border

SECOND FEMALE WORKER.
And our sons they too should stay behind
the ones who plow the field and dig the mine
They're not allowed to learn to read and write
Want to keep them ignorant so they'll never see the light

SINGER.
Fourth scene in which
Hölderlin has
a master of rhetoric
confirm his views
for which he must then bear
the consequences
when he expresses them

Enter Hölderlin. Sinclair and Schmid approach him.
Warm embraces.

SINGER.
Hölderlin refusing to acknowledge his defeat
promptly enrolls at the university where he will meet
old friends who whisk him off to hear a professor
derided by many by many praised In his lecture
he explains the need the necessity for revolution
His name is Fichte His entrance is greeted with
    commotion

*Fichte, meanwhile, has entered. Several Students stamp
their feet. There is also some hissing and booing. Fichte
mounts the platform. The Workers exit.*

FICHTE.
The right to revolution is a basic human right
and this right becomes a duty
when a state
flagrantly contradicts
its purpose
Composed of individuals the state should
as an entity be nothing more
than a compact of free and
independent individuals whose activities
are subject only to
their private code of ethics
In no wise then nor in any way
may the state restrict them
or coerce
being but a means
to bring these individuals
closer to
the ideal society
To support the individual
so that each may educate himself
and use his talents
to his best advantage
attention to this task alone
is the point and meaning of the state which
in turn must strive
to make itself superfluous
as must the government as well
For the aim of each of these must be

to function only for a time
then decree its own abolishment

SCHMID.
As if there were such individuals
free to decide and
act as they see fit
On what grounds then do you justify
the individual's right
to overthrow his government

FICHTE.
No other than
one's self
can rule over
the individual
No other than
my own self
better knows
what is within me
And while no change
can be observed unless
brought about by my own action
and while all things remain unchanged
if I fail to act
only what I myself determine
can be law and duty

SCHMID.
Rousseau also talked about
free individuals
and their uniting
in a social contract
but we know what kind of contract

to this day
obtains in our society
Each fights against the other
with uncontrolled savagery
to enrich himself

FICHTE.
Rousseau limited himself to pointing out
degeneration
and did not waste his strength
recommending ways
for its elimination
Rousseau was full of energy indeed
but of one kind only
the energy of suffering
He showed us there was reason in stillness
But only through struggle
can the reasoned will to action emerge
We exist as individuals
only to act
That is what Rousseau failed to see

SCHMID.
If every individual has the right
to rise up in revolt
then every counter-revolutionary
has the same right
which is how the emigrés from France
could justify the measures taken
to bring down the National Assembly

FICHTE.
The individual who revolts against the state
remains a rebel and cannot be compared

to a people who give expression to their hate
of their oppressors by rising up to bring them down
Only the people as a whole possess the right
to stage a revolution
I repeat
whenever a state shall break its pledge
its power to rule must be broken
A case in point would be
where privileged classes
oppress the common people

SINCLAIR.
In every nation in Europe

FICHTE.
And in such case obsolete contracts granting privileges
    to
church or aristocracy must be torn up and give way to
    the new

SINCLAIR.
And if the ruling class resist
and resort to every means at their disposal
to hunt us down

FICHTE.
The situation then is one wherein
to throw off all self-styled authorities
force is justified
for the right to revolution
by its very nature includes
the use of revolutionary force

Some Students start fighting. A scuffle, a brawl.

SCHMID.
But where there is property
there is also possession of weapons
so all we can do is to gape at the sight
of the possessors' overwhelming might
They won't be quick to run away of course
even if we threaten to resort to force

SINGER.
Because they're cracking down on revolutionaries
friend Hiller goes under an assumed name these days
Calls himself Siegfried Schmid But what's in a name
His politics and haircut remain the same
Hiller stirred up a fine political stew
Now the Jacobin Schmid takes a turn at it too

The commotion increases. Fichte's voice rises over the noise.

FICHTE.
No state
not even the most brutal
is unalterable
Wherever rulers scorn justice they may justly
be regarded as mankind's enemy
and each one of us must then rise
to overthrow those who tyrannize

A group of German nationalist students has started to sing.

CHORUS OF NATIONALIST STUDENTS.
And so we saw the sansculottes
with death and the devil hatch their plot
grabbing and stealing whatever they could
and dug their own grave by their greed
The common man robbed by the headstone stood
and the great Revolution was over for good

A STUDENT.

Just as France was filled with looting brigands
German thieves are looting their way through German
    lands
What people earned by the sweat of their brow
is legally theirs or so they claim now

CHORUS OF NATIONALIST STUDENTS.

And chaos and anarchy everywhere
spread through the country as never before
No time for philosophical discussion
now everyone's trying to save his own skin
As for false prophets demagogues and that lot
it's time to beat them up and throw them out

A STUDENT.

All this revolution talk is ridiculous
Germany awake It's time to clean house
Time to make order
Time to drive the red rabble out of the country and over
    the border

A student writes on the blackboard in capital letters
GERMANY AWAKE! Schmid promptly goes to the black-
board. He erases the words. Students jump on him.

SCHMID.

How now Herr Professor
out of this society
should a common will
come to be

FICHTE.

The solution will not simply present
itself but must be searched for
along the path to enlightenment

We would be grossly in error
if we were to commit
a single daring act
that would result not in improvement
in the commonweal
but would more likely be an unspeakable burden to one
    and all
True Most national constitutions are defective
and protection of inalienable human rights ineffective
Still
all we need to do
is to be patient and not give cause for further blame
Consider from the princes' point of view
how difficult it is to introduce new
principles Therefore we
are duty-bound as academics to pursue
the search for truth and then devotedly
to spread the truth as wide as possible
each within his own large circle
Gentlemen
while the worth and dignity of freedom
must rise up from below
liberation can only come
from above

SINCLAIR.
Even if we made ourselves
worthy of freedom
the monarchs would never
give us freedom

FICHTE.
Do not believe it
No prince could bear

to turn a deaf ear
to calls for justice
or to spurn justice altogether

SCHMID.
You extol the right
of revolution
and now delude yourself
claiming that
the power of the state
which is the bastion
of the ruling class
will at our command
blow itself up
You proclaimed the right
to revolutionary power
and now you engage
in demagoguery
to have the government
which serves to protect
the rights of the ruling class
without a struggle
give up the ghost

FICHTE.
Our goal is to change things for the better
Our examination
however
of what can presently be done
shows that a solid foundation
has yet to be built
on which to base a revolution

SCHMID.
So then
the idea that must come
from the people
must now be given
to the people

FICHTE.
A people
does not yet exist
Only day labourers and ragged apprentices
loafing and roving in desolate lands
crofters and cottagers stranded in villages
farmhands and maids weary with working
and though great is their outrage and indignation
they still lack a common voice
Under the conditions of these our days
only the educated middle class
is ready to consolidate
and join forces with the progressive nobility
and united compel
the feudal overlords and princes
to introduce reform
and alleviate the misery of the people

*A Student writes on the blackboard: UNIVERSISTAS
ORDINIS IMPERANTIS ANCILLA.*

*During the renewed outbreak of beatings an Officer and a
Troop of Gendarmes enter.*

FICHTE.
Gentlemen
Do not forget
that you as representatives

of the noble mind and worthiness
have an obligation
to strive for exemplary governance
within
first of all
the German nation
then following our example
Europe as a whole
until
all continents
are at last transformed into
a mighty empire
ruled by philosophers

SCHMID.
So
after all the shouting
philosophy makes
common cause
with the police

CHORUS OF ELITE STUDENTS.
And we reject a state
that exists only as an illusion
and of which to be a citizen
is no cause for pride but for disgrace
The state we hold up in its place
is one led by an elite
that treats its enemy
as it deserves

*The Gendarmes seize Hölderlin, Schmid, Sinclair, and a
couple of other Students who are picked out as guilty by the
German Nationalists and shoved forward.*

CHORUS OF ELITE STUDENTS.
And we no longer want our country to be divided
and conquered by foreign races
We would throw out the Levantine
and the Latinate crew
the decadent French and above all the Jew
so that at last the German people
may at last be healed and blossoming reveal
what long has lain hidden in the Teutonic soul

The Gendarmes violently drive the arrested men into a cluster.

FIRST STUDENT.
They deny Professor Fichte highly respected
his right to teach the course they elected

SECOND STUDENT.
They are members all
of a group that's called
the Band of the Equals

THIRD STUDENT.
They want to overthrow
the nobility

FOURTH STUDENT.
Want to establish
a democratic
German republic

OFFICER.
We're arresting you
Purpose investigation
of your identity

The Gendarmes handcuff the group in pairs.

FIRST STUDENT.
Hang them
Off to the lanterns with them

The Gendarmes push the arrested men ahead of them.

SCHMID.
Show your sharp blade
Sinclair

HÖLDERLIN.
O Edward o Edward
why does your shoe
so drip with blood

SINCLAIR.
O I have killed
my father dear

*As the Gendarmes lead off the arrested men, the German
nationalist students gather around Fichte, who stands
dumbfounded behind the lectern.*

CHORUS OF NATIONALIST STUDENTS.
If you haven't heard yet now's the time
Germany's hour is bound to come
United here in Europe's heart
we shall rid our nation of rabble and rot
Marching forward with banners unfurled
we shall be masters of the entire world

*Hölderlin, the last among the prisoners, suddenly tries to
wrench himself free. He is overpowered by the Gendarmes
and dragged off, still attached to the other prisoner by the
handcuffs.*

SINGER.

This scene brings to the fore
the poet and the philosopher
which is why there's more talk about
teachers and visionary preachers
than farmers and the down-and-out
the latter of which simply disappear
when those who seek the sublime appear
To be sure the art of Goethe and Schiller
signaled the dawn of a whole new age
in which science and education took centre stage
although neither had the insight to grasp
that only the great and populous mass
the common people can bring to fruition
the great upheaval the revolution
Thus too it was that the solution formulated
by Johann Gottlieb Fichte was relegated
to academic limbo and his revolutionary gospel
regarded as purely theoretical
His ego stands upright his freedom-loving I
while freedom's pickpockets multiply
Instead of acting himself he can only look on
as the alternative world continues to spin
and his influence fades into oblivion
His patriotic theses are quickly tainted
by nationalist students who marched and ranted
and brawling spreads like unleashed hounds
the German misery growing by leaps and bounds

Scene 5

Clipped bushes and hedges suggest a park. In the background, guests and the homeowners appear and disappear. A constant coming and going. Quick entrances, rapid changes in the groupings. Music distant and coming closer. Everything reminiscent of a Totentanz.

Merchant Gogel and Banker Bethmann enter.

SINGER.
Fifth scene in which
Hölderlin though
in his thoughts far ahead
of his time
must submit to the demands
of the present until
the conflict
leads
to a violent
solution

GOGEL.
I have tried to read
a piece by this tutor Hölderlin
published in
the *Literary Journal*
But it's all nonsense
Don't understand
how such stuff finds
a publisher

BETHMANN.
He looks so depressed
and anxious
since the reviewers

dismissed him
Schlegel says
that what Hölderlin passes off
as poetry
is sheer pretension and rubbish
And Kotzebue
speaks of absurdly versified
drivel

GOGEL.
As for Hegel
in service in my home
I have nothing but praise for him
Even Herr von Goethe
thinks highly of him
and often engages
him in conversation

Gogel and Bethmann exit. Enter Hölderlin, Schmid, and Sinclair.

Sinclair in the formal clothing of a princely official, Schmid in torn clothing, with a wild mane.

Hölderlin in the simple apparel of a house tutor.

SINCLAIR.
People like you
in every age
have a pack of mangy dogs
snapping at their heels
whining and howling

SCHMID.
Critics are
privy rats

They avenge themselves
on us for being
unable to create
anything themselves

HÖLDERLIN.
So I write
for those who destroy
deface and defile
When will I reach
those I seek
those who can see
pure of eye
those who can hear
with open ear

SCHMID.
It always amuses me
this ambition
to leave behind
some verses.
Sometimes yes
a few lines come to mind
but it's enough for me
to let them just flash by
Anyway when the day comes
there'll be no more singing

*Schmid and Sinclair exit. Hölderlin remains behind,
impatiently waiting.*

SINGER.
September seventeen hundred ninety-eight:
at Adlerflucht the country estate
ringed with boxwood blackthorn wild rose

which snatch and tear at strollers' clothes
scratch lovers' hands that seek to pass
letters through hedges to arrange meeting places
where they can unite at least briefly
until their overwrought behavior gives them away
And so with tears and sighs it's over ended.
and they must part as fate intended

*Enter Susette Gontard. In the background, meanwhile,
eavesdropping, Margarete Gontard. Susette breathless.*

SUSETTE GONTARD.
As soon as the guests depart
come to me by the back entry
Run up the steps quickly
The door will be open as always
The children should be in the downstairs
blue room by then and if anyone
should see you that's no matter
Hardly remarkable if two people
who live under the same roof
should spend half an hour together

HÖLDERLIN.
We can't do that.

SUSETTE GONTARD.
O when you talk like that
I feel so numbed beloved
I would gladly give you a heaven

HÖLDERLIN.
Impossible

SUSETTE GONTARD.

Even when I seem dead
and dry
I still burn within
I have you in me
Holder
constantly
and against this passion
I must like you
defend myself.

HÖLDERLIN.

And live a life of resignation
and melancholy.

SUSETTE GONTARD.

You know that we can never
on this earth
belong to one another
To seek to do so
would be folly
For us there is only
the sweet pain
and this
with tears
will inwardly
more
strongly bind us

HÖLDERLIN.

Forget it

He turns away abruptly. Susette hurries on.

SINGER.

Hölderlin spent nearly three years
in the house of Gontard
Again unable as a poet to keep alive
he's forced to play the tutor to survive
must repeat the 'prenticeship with young Henri
which at accurséd Waltershausen he botched deplorably

*Enter Henry Gontard, same actress as the one who played
Fritz von Kalb.*

HENRY GONTARD.

So here you are
in the garden
with the guests
I looked for you everywhere
Father told me
you would be in the kitchen
helping to carry the baskets
and trays

HÖLDERLIN.

Yes
that's what I was hired to do

HENRY GONTARD.

Holder
Are we going to go for an evening stroll again
with mamam
and will you recite poems for us
in the arbour

*From the distance, the call: Henri Henri (French pronun-
ciation) Henry rushes off. Hölderlin exits.*

Enter Merchant Schellenberg and Margarete Gontard

SCHELLENBERG.
What is ailing Frau Susette
She looks so pale
and poorly.
Her brother should
send her off to the spa again

MARGARETE GONTARD.
Everything is so unsettled
all around us In Taunus one never knows
when one might encounter the French army
while south of here
all the talk is of revolution

SCHELLENBERG.
It's been a long time since
you've been here with us
For you gracious lady
who take such pleasure in bestowing gifts
I have ordered a shipment
of meerschaum pipes

SINGER.
At Schellenberg's establishment
you'll find jewels rings and ornament
some small but still quite beautiful
the sort of gift that has proven useful
for sustaining friendships and suitable
for keeping love from growing cool

MARGARETE GONTARD.
We scarcely dare
go into the city any more

with all the attacks
taking place in plain daylight

SCHELLENBERG.
Ach ja Our good name
as trade metropolis
will soon be lost
It's high time the senate
provided more constables

Schellenberg and Margarete Gontard exit.
Enter Hölderlin, Schmid, Sinclair.

HÖLDERLIN.
And if I were to leave here
where would I go then
I always hear my mother saying
choose a steady job
with a family
and a secure position
in society
As if one's duty
to one's own work
were nothing
as if my *Hyperion*
were nothing

SCHMID.
You weren't cut out to be
a schoolmaster
Strange
Not like our Hegel
who manages to combine
the useful with the comfortable

by not only steeping
himself in his phenomenal self-awareness
but also in
his employer's wine cellar
Nor will you ever
end up as a diplomat
like Sinclair
who has crept up the ass
of the Count of Homburg

SINCLAIR.
You understand nothing
about the higher politics.
I made my nest
inside the court
so I could blow up
the whole despotic regime

SCHMID.
How can it succeed here
when in Paris
all that's left of
the revolutionary violence
is a burgher's fart
The Messers Jourdan and
Tallyrand
have long since sold out
the German revolutionaries
All they want to do
is to pacify the princes
and bring them under
their control

SINCLAIR.

If we can't win the Directorate
over to our side
we'll have to do it
on our own
At the congress to be held
in Rastatt
there are many of us
who support the overthrow
of Württemberg
even if this
would bring us
in opposition to France

SCHMID.

Because nothing will happen
and I cannot any longer endure this tedium
and because I am a man of the extremes
I'm leaving
either
for the island of Tahiti
where even in winter the flowers bloom
or
to join up with the army
of Duke Karl
mustering now in Helvetia
so
when the snow falls
they can dye it red

HÖLDERLIN.
And what is left for me to do

SCHMID.
Spirits of the air
Spirits of the caves
Wings
thundering

Hölderlin, Schmid, Sinclair exit.

*Two Maids enter, straining under the weight of the heavy
baskets they are carrying, one full of wine bottles, the other
of fruit.*

FIRST MAID.
I can't take time for the little one
I'm so bursting with milk
that my clothes are soaked

She sets down the basket, rubs her breasts.

FIRST MAID.
O it's so painful

SECOND MAID.
Come on Quick
We're sure to get a good tip
today.

Both exit, carrying the baskets.

Susette Gontard and Hölderlin reappear.

SUSETTE GONTARD.
Better if you don't come
They're keeping close watch on us
I fear
Wait until it's dark
Then we'll meet

by the chestnut tree.
I hear that you've been ordered
to serve as coachman for the guests
It's my Jacob's wish

HÖLDERLIN.
Groom horses
Clean boots
Run to market
If only I could put to better use
the energy
I waste in hatred
for that rich table
on whose crumbs
I still depend

SUSETTE GONTARD.
Don't let yourself be distracted by him
who cannot see your genius
and only knows
how to handle money

HÖLDERLIN.
And who supports us all
You handsomely
for me
coarse kicks

SUSETTE GONTARD.
Be still beloved
We must be careful
to keep things in balance
and not neglect
our duties.

HÖLDERLIN.
I have played the cringing servant
in order to protect you
have always behaved as if
I was intent on every task
as if I was made to be
a ball that men and things
can play with
My life is still nothing
but a blundering
Always these attacks
of colic lurk attack
without forewarning
I stagger and collapse
Sometimes I get up
Sometimes I swoon
and faint
Susette
it must end

SUSETTE GONTARD.
Were you to leave
I would drown
in night and death
It is you who holds me up
who have shown me the way
to beauty

HÖLDERLIN.
Quickly in the bushes then
to embrace
a fleeting kiss
and then alone
to burst

Suzette hurries away. Hölderlin crumples, falls, writhes in cramps.

The First Maid returns. Bends over him.

FIRST MAID.
What's wrong then

Hölderlin moans, presses his hand against his abdomen.
The Maid helps him up.

FIRST MAID.
I think
it was ambition to be one of them
the educated
that knocked you over
You ought to be just one of us
and not think you're too good
to help out
with the serving

She brushes off his clothing. Supports him and exits with him.

Gontard enters, arm in arm with Suzette.

Merchant Gogel and Hegel accompany them.

SINGER.
Jakob Gontard
the capital in his big store alone worth
five hundred thousand gulden
Uncountable
the money running through his fingers
at the bank
Wholesale-merchant Gogel
five million guldens' worth

financing imports business commissions
wine liquors and perfumes

GONTARD.
Ach you see my dear Gogel
while my merchant-house brings in
sufficient for my daily needs
such an enterprise cannot be compared
to the energizing effect
created by the bank
which pulses and flows
like a living organism
not merely in transactions of exchange
for all such monies as trade fairs require
nor in deposits or in form of loans
but above all
on a world-wide scale
I am somewhat concerned
however by the storms
I see spreading through the commercial world
and the political as well
to which prominent firms
have already fallen victim

GOGEL.
My motto is
the strong
must become stronger
Business would flourish
if we could catch up with
the Netherlanders
and British
and with our own ships
bring the colonial goods

from abroad which now
creates such difficulties
for our merchants

HEGEL.
True enough Herr von Gogel
It was the Revolution
that gave money
its expansive power.
The opening up
of foreign markets
is the precondition
for the growth of
the modern industrial state
And not only
do we see increasing prosperity
in those European lands
devastated by the war
but there is also the humane view
of the weak and formless
people of the Orient
to whom we bring enlightenment

GONTARD.
Then there are those
who begrudge us
our ambitious projects
and dream instead
of granting power to the people
in the true sense
counter-revolutionaries

HEGEL.
Well said
Sir

Inventiveness
boldness of enterprise
now lead our world
toward
its highest level of organization
So General Buonaparte
in Egypt now
shows that France
is on the way
to grabbing hold of her share
It would be foolish
to ignore
the imperial trend of our time

Gontard, Susette, Gogel, and Hegel exit.

Enter two Gardeners, one with a rake, the other with a basketful of leaves.

FIRST WORKER.
One thing I don't understand
There are a lot more of our kind
than theirs here in the park
Why do we have to let them
push us around

SECOND WORKER.
That's because they've
wrung our necks so long
that our tongues stick out
and we bellow as loud
as if we were their cattle

Enter Bethmann and Susette Gontard. The Workers doff their caps and bow deeply. The Bethmann and Susette pay no heed.

The Workers exit.

BETHMANN.
The splendid autumn air
the pruned trees and
Greek sculptures
here in your park
stir the muse in me
When all is said and done
of all that we possess
art alone endures

SINGER.
This Herr von Bethmann
a banker and a statesman too
is popularly called
Le Roi de Francfort
Medals are showered on his chest
by a government deeply in debt to him
having borrowed from him to pay for its wars
As he himself goes on to say

BETHMANN.
Greed has never been
the motive of my enterprise
Above all else
I place the advancement
of the arts
and gentility

SUSETTE GONTARD.
Nor do I know
of another house than yours
in which

cultural treasures
gather in such number

BETHMANN.
A fortune and success
these are the prerequisites
of virtue

SUSETTE GONTARD.
Poverty has always been
detrimental
to good morals

BETHMANN.
Discriminating taste
understanding and friendship
are brought forth by wealth

Susette Gontard and Bethmann exit.

*Hölderlin enters, carrying bottles and a tray of glasses.
Schmid, half-drunk, accompanies him.*

HÖLDERLIN.
Horrible how they
murdered Babeuf and
Buonarotti still
lies in prison because
they wouldn't admit
that the Revolution
had failed

SCHMID.
Those who admit no compromise
the best thing to do
is to kill themselves

There's that great spokesman
for great heroic deeds
the extraordinarily private privy counselor
to whom all bend the knee
to kiss his boots
Think of it
This is the man
whose *Werther* once
moved us to tears

HÖLDERLIN.
Meanwhile I learn
carrying glasses so
learn how to reawaken
my flagging
strength
learn to balance
my way out of the gathering dusk
and above all
not to bury myself
in my sorrow
but to bury my sorrow itself
The Revolution
will start again
from the beginning
But first of all
the cause of the whole evil
the holy right
of private acquisition
must be swept away

Hölderlin and Schmid exit.
Goethe and Bethmann enter, and at some remove, Hegel.

GOETHE.
I have no fear
that this land will not
in time be united
Our good highroads
will do their part
and I think of the new
steam engines which in England
have been invented and
are said to roll on tracks
And so I foresee
the uniting of peoples
through locomotion
My formula for
future progress
is the evolution of pedagogy
plus steam engine

BETHMANN.
If only the rebelliousness
of the lower classes
would not prevent us
from instituting
social reform

Hegel has come up alongside Bethmann

HEGEL.
If Your Excellency permit
this discontent among the populace
could be remedied
if
as was intended for a time in France
the prospect were held out

that all might enjoy
the right to own property

BETHMANN.
But that's just it
They want to get their hands
on our money

HEGEL.
Yet it would suffice
to secure for them a bare
subsistence minimum
For were the craftsmen and
small tradesmen able
to accumulate their savings
it would be in their own interest
to see that order is maintained

BETHMANN.
Herr Doctor Hegel.
you have given me
an idea
We should not only
support large commercial firms
but also enable those
of modest means to put
their savings safely in a bank
and help them enjoy
receiving interest
Even the penny
put in proper circulation
can work for us

Bethmann, Goethe, and Hegel exit.
Enter Susette and Margarete Gontard.

SUSETTE GONTARD.
O Gretel Gretel
are you sure

MARGARETE GONTARD.
My brother knows everything.
He can no longer be restrained
and shall immediately
dismiss your Holder

SUSETTE GONTARD.
O God If only
the guests don't find out

MARGARETE GONTARD.
You can be glad if
he does not shoot him

SUSETTE GONTARD.
Yes He must go
No one must hear of it
The honor of the family
must be preserved

She starts to cry.

SUSETTE GONTARD.
O I feel so cold
I am so woven into him
that nothing can
separate me from him
and what binds us
will not cease
in this short life
To love as I love him
nobody will love him again

and to love me as strongly as he does
he will never love anything again

Margarete embraces Susette, who is sobbing.

SUSETTE GONTARD.
It's to please him that today
I wear this lilac-white dress
Had it made exactly
according to his taste
O Gretel Gretel
you must bring
my letters to him as before
and tell him too
that on the first Thursday
of the month
at nine o'clock at night
he must appear
under the chestnut tree
I only want to see
with my own eyes
that he is still alive
and well

Susette and Margarete Gontard exit.

SINGER.
We'll watch the farewell only since it the most
    dramatic part
was what set most tongues wagging from the start
and we'll skip over those stolen hours spent
in Susette's room or beneath a starry firmament
Nor shall we to that endless prattle pay more heed
about what both knew would never satisfy their need
but shall observe their pleasure wither as perforce

the garden party runs its stately course
with its Frankfort kings of finance and for show
a scattering of literati strolling to and fro

Goethe and Hegel appear.

GOETHE.
What sort of prehistoric
monster may that be

Hölderlin and Schmid approaching them.

SCHMID.
It is the poet Siegfried Schmid
proud to admit
he marches with those great gray masses
unrecognized as yet by the upper classes
but who will one day rise to overthrow
those of you who cannot see us now

GOETHE.
But there is also
that young Hölderlin
I read your booklet
about Hyperion
and found it
not without some merit
but it often seemed to me
that your depiction of nature
came not from
feeling and inner
contemplation
but was more often
merely a matter
of imitation and
hearsay

HÖLDERLIN.
No   Hellas
this Greece is not
It is but a small piece of
my own land's
distant brightness
whose presence
is hidden
in dusk and darkness
I have never been in Greece
Here though I have been all too long
and my invocation of Greece
is a call for the destruction
of the miserable drudgery
in which we hourly
degrade ourselves

Goethe raises his hands to stop Hölderlin from going on.

HÖLDERLIN.
This land
it is a dung heap
I want to unload
my hate
for those stove-stoking bootlicking
parasitical hangers-on
of our princes
who luxuriate
in the corpse stench
of spilled life's blood
And if the world were
in one rare glimpse of spring
to rid itself of its sorrow
and to break the chains

of every slave
each here would remain
in his own slot
concerned only with
the weather
We are strangers
in our own house
and sit at the gate
like Ulysses
with his beggar's staff
while the shameless suitors
riot in the halls
and ask who
brought us this wayfarer

*Goethe turns away. Hölderlin and Schmid approach
Goethe and Hegel.*

HÖLDERLIN.
I long for the day when
I shall throw the pen
into the rubbish
and let the pages flutter loose
in the wind
and go
where I am needed

Hölderlin stomps off, followed by Schmid.

GOETHE.
What makes these Holterlings
and Schmids
so subjectivistically overwrought
Is it the empirical world
in which they live

that has had this unfortunate effect
on their romantic inclination
You Doctor Hegel
were a fellow student
I believe

HEGEL.
No other
has stimulated
my thought
as Hölderlin
I have incorporated
various of his visions into
my system of the rational
Yet no other
is so vulnerable
to crushing pressures
A single word
uttered at random
or in passing
wounds him to the heart
The world
will utterly
destroy him

GOETHE.
Yet why must these Schmids
and Hölderlins
wear such manes and
such grim looks
Their outward appearance
is as unkempt and barbaric
as their language
Have you noticed

the remarkable grimaces
into which Schmid twists
his mouth
I think one could
perceive in them
the brutality
of the epoch twitching

Goethe and Hegel exit.

SINGER.
It was a time when people talked a lot
about the good the true the beautiful
lofty concepts long since hollowed out by rot
mocking the cruelty and poverty that were the rule

*Gontard with Hölderlin come forward. Gontard very softy
and with restrained anger.*

GONTARD.
So you'll pack your things
and be gone
today
You'll be given your wages
for the month

*Gontard exits. Immediately thereafter, Henry Gontard
appears.*

HENRY GONTARD.
Holder
what will become of me
and all you've taught me
when you're gone

He tugs Hölderlin's sleeve. Holds up a little package.

HENRY GONTARD.

You must send me word
of where you are
so I can visit you
Here's a little present from mama
tobacco for your pipe

*Henry hugs him. Hölderlin lifts him up. For a moment
they stand so. Then Henry tears himself free, runs off.*

*From the background, the guests step forward, Ladies and
Gentlemen. They form three choruses.*

In the first chorus: Jakob, Susette, and Margarete Gontard.

In the second chorus: Schellenberg and Gogel.

In the third chorus: Bethmann.

*To the side stand Hölderlin, Schmid, and Sinclair. Sinclair
has his arm around Hölderlin's shoulder. Across from them,
Goethe and Hegel.*

FIRST CHORUS.

We march toward the blissful golden age
The little shop the workman's shed
shall be transformed into vast halls
to house the mechanized division of labour.
And from the cellars women and children
shall some streaming out to work the looms and
in the mills and with their ill-paid labour ease their
     hunger
O how the pistons pound the great wheels turn
and smoke billows endless from the factory stacks
as the glistening pistons pound
We lend invest
and collect on both with interest

ALL CHORUSES.
And ever higher through our enterprise
our stock exchange quotations rise

SCHMID.
Seething and hissing in its own grease
growing greedier as the years pass
Capital towers like a colossus above us
We condemned it to death but still it rises
never bolder or more ruthless
than in this year of our lord

SECOND CHORUS.
Provincial exchanges become trade corporations
with branches across this and other nations
Gentle dark-skinned natives bring in the harvest
The corporations take care of the rest
Coffee and tobacco from Batavia
Tea from Macao rubber from Siam
from India cotton and silk
peppercorns cinnamon cloves from Malaya
O how the ships steam through the oceans
and how the warehouses and treasuries fill
We attach foreclose and confiscate
and our stocks shower us
with dividends

ALL CHORUSES.
And ever higher through our enterprise
our stock exchange quotations rise

SCHMID.
A rotten pigsty the whole of Europe
and northern America too
They cast their nets around the world

to haul in treasures and more slaves
Those plunderers have taken over everywhere
to rule by crucifix fire and sword

THIRD CHORUS.
Our small smithies
with anvil and bellows
will become foundries
with giant casting moulds
clanging ovens and in our employ
armies of the best men
drawn from the people to produce
with artful skill
cannon barrels steel plate
and wagons full of bombs of all sizes
round and smooth
O god and business Daily the world demands
more iron
We plan produce and fix the rate
accrue get rich accumulate

ALL CHORUSES.
And ever higher through our enterprise
our stock exchange quotations rise

*As the third Chorus starts to speak, the Servant Women
and Farm Workers enter. Other Workers follow them,
miners, factory hands, and industrial workers.*

Silently they come forward in their ragged clothing.

*Finally, as a great group coming together, they completely
block from view the Choruses in the background.*

*Only Hölderlin, Sinclair, and Schmid are to be seen
among them.*

Act II

Scene 6

Chairs and a large table. Stacks of book, piles of papers. On the walls in the background, maps of regions of the earth.

A dais for the chorus.

Present are Hölderlin, Hegel, Neuffer, Schelling, Schmid, Sinclair, the Glazier Wagner, the Singer.

Schmid in torn uniform.

The friends are greeting each other.

SINGER.
Scene six in which
Hölderlin expounds to his assembled friends
the theme of his drama Empedocles
in the course of which is seen
what binds him still
with these with whom
he set out long ago

The guests sit around the table. Wagner serves them a meal.

Hölderlin does not sit. He gathers his thoughts for his lecture, and then, as he speaks, he walks agitatedly back and forth.

One by one and almost imperceptibly, members of the Chorus appear: they are the actors who play the Male and Female Workers.

The speaker for Hermokrates: same actor as the one who played Duke Karl Eugen.

The speaker for Pánthea: same actress as the one who played Wilhelmine Kirms.

The assignment of the Chorus is to expand Hölderlin's own vision and voice. For the audience, the Chorus is not there. They understand that what the Chorus says is spoken by Hölderlin himself.

The manner in which certain names are accented in the Empedocles drama reflects Hölderlin's usage.

SINGER.
Seventeen hundred ninety-nine's the year
and a November Homburg-by-the-Hill's the setting where
oppressed by cares and by critics ill-used
the poet with Glazier Wagner is housed
His novel *Hyperion* has just been printed
but neither it nor his great odes have dinted
his need   If it weren't for his mother and his friend Sinclair
he would be in the street with a cup like a beggar
Neuffer from his parish comes well-fed
Schelling from Jena recently promoted
to full professor   He's found his niche.
Hegel too is well-off if not rich
has climbed the ladder of society
inherited money serving as his entrée
Thus this erstwhile tutor can stay at home
to work at leisure on his epochal tome
So most of those assembled here have stepped

sedately up and settled down except
Siegfried Schmid who as a lowly dragoon
will have to touch a comrade for a gulden soon
to return to barracks For all that this exception owns
apart from his uniform is his skin and bones

SCHELLING.
And why has our foremost revolutionary
joined the army of the Archduke Karl
thereby exposing himself to that most dubious of all fates
to die for the fatherland

SCHMID.
Because the battle now
is against that arch-traitor
to the Revolution Buonaparte.
The German Jacobins are
as grossly swindled by this dictator
as are the Jacobins of Paris
No sooner does he flee the shadows of the pyramids
the sphynx's mocking laughter still ringing in his ears
than all he can think of is
to gulp down Europe whole

HEGEL.
He ranks with Caesar
Alexander
In the will of such great figures
the world's own spirit finds expression
clairvoyantly perceiving
what the times call for
Such men perceive emerging forces
ripe for development
and boldly seize them

HÖLDERLIN.
A monster is what he is

HEGEL.
I call him a hero
His strides
will stamp
the coming century

HÖLDERLIN.
Will trample it

HEGEL.
His main intent is to establish
a strong state
The state is the guardian of the law
Where the rule of law obtains
reason too is found

HÖLDERLIN.
It used to be that theory served
you as a battering ram
to break down the doors
of reality
Now
solely to support your theory
you build yourself a state
impregnable to all attack

SCHMID.
Of course
Because he's after a professor's chair
like Schelling's

HEGEL.
I stand on the terra firma
of established fact
while you and Holder both
teeter on the verge
of throwing yourselves away
It's because you can see
no way out
of your utter lack of hope
that the pistol's crack
attracts you
while Holder is exalted to such heights
he loses sight
of himself

NEUFFER.
And both as well look
pale and ragged

HEGEL.
Holder's only just had
his one day a month
when off he lopes 'cross hill and dale
to Frankfort to inhale
beneath the chestnut trees
the essence of his fair Diotima.
Meanwhile Buonaparte
has prepared his coup d'état.

NEUFFER.
And I was so delighted Holder
to think you'd shaken off Susette at last

HEGEL.
O no He still needs
his goddess
to sublimate his lechery

SINGER.
Why nip and snarl at each other so
We are gathered here as you well know
to learn what lasting and substantial theme
this man has found within the rubble of our time
It's not asking too much to let him have his say
and to give us a report about his play

The Chorus starts immediately.

CHORUS.
Who is Empedócles

HÖLDERLIN.
The mortal enemy
of all one-sided being
He hates servility
and sham
despises those
who fear for their own skin and
tremble at the thought
of losing office

CHORUS.
Where lives Empedócles

HÖLDERLIN.
The land in which he lives
is ruled by priests and scribes
a land in which all that's free
spontaneous is forbidden

and every deed finds itself
hemmed in
by restrictions

CHORUS.
Where is this land

HÖLDERLIN.
It is where
beyond the city and the fields
all is barren
where scorched steppes
rise to mountains
whose highest peak
a vast volcano
lies in cloud
I call it Aetna
and the country's name is
Agrigento

CHORUS.
And in what year is this

HÖLDERLIN.
Five hundred years before
our calendar began
and now.

CHORUS.
Why so remote
and such a place

HÖLDERLIN.
Because a mythic figure
must appear
now

when the great Revolution's fire
has been put out
and flickers only
among a scattered few
Because one man
weary of counting the hours
must remind us
that something that once glowed red
and sank into
the immeasurable past
can once again
with mighty breath
become a living flame

CHORUS.
And how will this man
prove that

HÖLDERLIN.
By an act of voluntary
resolution
in which he is not content
with the idea alone
but bursts out from it
gives up all
that habit custom
and the law require
and points to
the essential
He
philosopher and naturalist
master architect and skilled physician
chosen by many to be king
renounces all honours and

all ties
embodies in himself
the terrifying unexpected
which can for him
mean annihilation

HEGEL.
Why then does he not
remain within his nation Agrigento
and by virtue of his high office
act to change things for the better

HÖLDERLIN.
Because that nation
has grown so rigid
that nothing
but the extraordinary act
can shake it

HEGEL.
He could let himself
be crowned king

HÖLDERLIN.
The age of kings
is over

SCHMID.
And of the individual
as well
The masses' time has come

HÖLDERLIN.
Now all lies listless lifeless
corrupted by the high priests'
litanies

falsified the books for those
capable of reading
Every word
that's uttered
in the hierarchies
of the ruling civil servants
is a lie
What then can those who labour
in stores and workshops do
who fear to lose beneath the bludgeon
what little they may earn
And behold the peasantry
denied all education
since time began
superstitiously believes
that it is fated to know nothing
but eternal drudgery
With his bold step
he rouses them from their lethargy

CHORUS.
And where does this step
take him

HÖLDERLIN.
Away from the city
and from its hoarded
wealth
up through the fields and hills
to Aetna

NEUFFER.
As if it were Olympus

HEGEL.
He will not be missed

HÖLDERLIN.
Only thus
does he begin to live.

SCHELLING.
His tendency to act so unpredictably
will be exploited by his enemies
As soon as his intentions become known
they will rush in to fill his vacant place
They will hurl curses at him
and will decree
his banishment

CHORUS.
We hear this of Empedócles
Much has he done
building new roads and
channeling rivers
To the fields he brought
ingenious irrigation
combated epidemics
with his medicines
Tirelessly he worked
to instruct
the young

HÖLDERLIN.
And as you wait
Hermokrátes the high priest
prepares
to denounce him

SCHMID.

And he will present
the exemplary step
to the citizens as such a grievous offense
that they cannot grasp
and blinded
turn away from him

The speaker who represents Hermokrátes steps forward.

HERMOKRÁTES.

He is a heretic
Repudiates the age-honoured laws
Thinks himself wiser
than the high council
of the temple
Blasphemes
against the holy gods
sacrilegiously
seals a pact
with the elements
Woe to him
who would yet
accord respectful hearing
to a word he says
or who shelters him
when he comes
by night to the door
and to him who
when he dies
prepares the flame for his grave
He shall be banished do penance as an outcast
and perish in the wilderness
May floods and fires

winds and dust
devour him

GLAZIER WAGNER.
Does no one then
stand by him
Considering all he's done
he must surely have
friends and helpers
Where are they now

CHORUS.
Where are all those
who with him
planned projected
thoughtfully discussed
approved of his proposals
and to whose criticism
he stood open

SCHMID.
What a question
We know only too well
how quickly comrades turn
to worms and reptiles who
work their way into the wretched guts
of their fellow man and ravage him

HÖLDERLIN.
There is Strato
his brother
high-ranking citizen of Agrigento

CHORUS.
And what
does Strato say

SINCLAIR.
Strato says nothing.

GLAZIER WAGNER.
His own flesh and blood
He must hurry to help his brother

CHORUS.
Strato declines
The time he feels
is not ripe
He counsels
patience

SCHMID.
Like our Hegel

HEGEL.
The premature decision
may prove fatal
Suppression is inevitable
for the uprising
if it is proclaimed
when only a few
can follow
He becomes a murderer
who says too much
when silence is in order

HÖLDERLIN.
That is the voice
of my character
He will express himself
in just such words
in this tragedy

CHORUS.
Yet many of the young throughout the land
side with Empedócles
would be prepared at any time
and anywhere to join him

The speaker representing Pausánias steps forward.

PAUSÁNIAS.
How long must we wait
For centuries they have said
the time is not yet ripe
This can go on for another century
if we ourselves
do not bring it about

HÖLDERLIN.
Pausánias follows him
is his disciple and helper
sets out with him
for the mountains
to establish a camp
and there to train the warriors
who shall find the hard way up to them
so that later
they may bring renewal down
to Agrigento

GLAZIER WAGNER.
I still don't understand
why he doesn't gather those he trusts
around him in the city
There he could find hiding places weapons
could find provisions
with less trouble too

and the wounded
could be cared for
if it comes to that

HÖLDERLIN.
What lies ahead for him is
beyond description
grim and cold
This strange world and
the figures in it
whose like we
do not know as yet
I try
to bring them near to us
Listen closely
and perhaps what separates us
from this audacious matter
which took place so long ago
may yet be overcome

GLAZIER WAGNER.
He will come upon peasants herdsmen
who distrust and shun the city men
and for a piece of copper
will tell the mercenaries
which way he took and when.

CHORUS.
Night and day
Empedócles and Pausánias
have made their way
through fields and forests
Storm clouds were their roof
their bed black lava

Now all paths lie far behind them
and among the barren stones
prey is scant rare the kill
and weary on the heights
they find a pair of peasant huts

Out of the Chorus steps the Speaker of the Peasants.

PAUSÁNIAS.
We would like to buy
corn from you
and a gourd of water

THE PEASANT.
Some doors open for money.
not mine

PAUSÁNIAS.
We pay well

THE PEASANT.
Try elsewhere

PAUSÁNIAS.
A strip of cloth
to wrap around his feet
cut by the sharp stones
Look at him
On such a day as this
when the very beasts
seek caves to escape
the sun
don't make him stand outside

THE PEASANT.
I know him.

He's the man cursed and banished
from Agrigento
Be gone

SCHMID.
Yet by now surely
the partisans would already
be on the way
I would have joined them

CHORUS.
And the heavily armed cohorts have set out
secónded bodyguards otherwise assigned
to the priestly class and government officials
skilled in shooting stabbing cutting throats
trained in every form of torture
who set ablaze every hut they come upon
letting the women and children choke
to death on smoke and burn inside
and hang the wretched peasants from the trees

HEGEL.
Which viewed from an historical perspective
is only logical.
How else can they react
except with force
when the preservation of the state
is at stake
imperfect as that state may be

SINCLAIR.
But the viewpoint of this world-wise
character
can't be Strato's too
By now he must be wondering how

he can assist Empedócles
must know
that his brother
is counting on him

SCHELLING.
I imagine that by this time
the opinion of the people has become divided
the bold siding
with Empedócles
while Hermocrátes gathers around him
the easily-cowed multitude

SINGER.
A pity it is
that all
who love the hero
so long as he's in the ascendant
shun him
when he's lost his lustre and been deserted

CHORUS.
So attacked
by small green birds
whose sharp beaks
peck their skulls
through scorpion- and snake-infested thickets
and clouds of mosquitoes
gaunt with fever
and gasping for each breath
Empedócles
and at his side
Pausánias.

A VOICE FROM THE CHORUS.
Yet on the high plateau
a handful of field labourers
having left their hated masters
joins them
They bring a bony mule
to ease the long march
of Empedócles

ANOTHER VOICE FROM THE CHORUS.
Mere hope that someone had set out
of whom the whisper went
that he could improve our lot
this hope was enough
to make us leave our huts of clay
and with our sharp machetes
hack our way to him

CHORUS.
Then once again the thorny brush
wrong paths taken
the laborious turning back
thirst and hunger

HEGEL.
And was it for this then
that he took his daring leap
to offer himself up
as the most miserable
of the poor
and smash his dying head
upon the cliff

SCHELLING.
I begin

to understand
Empedócles' deed
as poetic action
for it is
in the creative act alone
that man defeats the evil
that resides in the darkest depths
within himself
and in the world

HEGEL.
Such an act of sacrifice
cannot move me
Whoever in an age
when tyrants are toppled
and states are overthrown
violently
takes his own life
cannot be regarded
as a leader of the people

SCHELLING.
We are speaking of poetry
Here we are freed
from the wretched need
to take united action
and we create instinctively
into infinity
It is only in art
I say
that we are capable
of totally
revolutionizing
our personality

HEGEL.
No one is granted wisdom
in his sleep
Instead of abstract striving
for limitless advance
I prefer setting
methodical
limits
Art
is only a stage
in the development of self-awareness
At some point art too will pass away
when reality
has reached completion

HÖLDERLIN.
Rumor of his march
has spread
In other regions
movements similar to his begin
Already there is talk
of resistance among the slaves
who work the silver mines
already there is talk
in the tense silence
of our cities
of a mighty army
gathering in the mountains

GLAZIER WAGNER.
But how is this pitiful band
of men that can barely
stand
supposed to help us

We are the ones who should go
and save those
up in the mountains

HÖLDERLIN.
Exactly so Wagner
For this is what Empedócles would say:
Rouse yourselves
from smugness
Do not expect to be helped
if you fail to help yourselves
Create your own time
and set out on your own path

SCHMID.
Strato must have managed
under cover of darkness
to get around the troops and
join Empedócles

CHORUS.
There is no sign of Strato
The little column slowly climbs
among the boulders
In the valleys far below
the pursuers' dogs are baying

A VOICE FROM THE CHORUS.
One of the slaves
drawn from the cattle farms
who
wandering with Empedócles
for several days became a free man
now lies dead
Flies lay their larvae

inside his swollen corpse
Those who continue on their way
bear the spear he brought

CHORUS.
But Pánthea
Pánthea
whom Empedócles
calls his sister
has long since left
her father Kritias
the priest
Dressed now in the garments
of one of her servant girls
her hair wrapped
in a ragged cloth
carrying a bundle
filled with
fruits and herbs
against malaria
and also with sharp
daggers
she has walked on country paths
through villages
unrecognized
and has arrived at last among the hills
where she now seeks her friend.

The Speaker for Pánthea steps out of the Chorus.

PÁNTHEA.
None of those
we hoped would rise
rose up

against the established authority
Those
who in their comfortable city offices
spoke of the necessity of the struggle
of the oppressed
now speak condescendingly
of Empedócles
who thinks
that this struggle
could be launched
from the desolate countryside

NEUFFER.
This too Holder
Would you really
set a woman down among
these men who have foresworn
not only
their allegiance to society
but all security and warmth as well

HÖLDERLIN.
She is his peer
She belongs to him
and he to her

CHORUS.
High among
Aetnas's sulfurous clouds
among the dark volcanic rocks
shivering
drinking the last few drops
of collected rain
retching from the tough

and rancid meat
of the slaughtered mule
his breathing laboured
behold Empedócles
racked with fever
his arms
his legs
swollen with edema

NEUFFER.
Stop
You've given us a hero
and sent him out into
a barren prehistoric world
ill-equipped
for deprivations
he must surely have foreseen
For provisions to reach him
he took no thought
His health is wretched
What then does he expect
From Pausánias
from all that ragtag crew
who joined them
but who lack all understanding
of his larger aim
he can scarcely hope for help
So plagued by diarrhoea
they squat behind bushes
What
I ask you
does he still have to hope for
up there on his Aetna

HÖLDERLIN.
He is neither mortally ill
nor stricken with despair
He is far more alive than many a man
who fancies himself as flourishing
What matter
that his teeth chatter in his head
Far sharper are his senses
than yours below
in Agrigento
who at fixed hours
spoon up your soup

HEGEL.
Even an allegory however
must have some logic
The way in which you show Empedócles
to us
makes him seem an addle-brained
Utopian
and yet
to judge by his position in society
he would have had
sufficient leisure
calmly and with forethought
to draw up his plan of action

HÖLDERLIN.
You
are the deluded ones
Can't you understand
that this fevered state this breathlessness
is your disease
which he must suffer

since in your stubbornness
you pit yourselves against his effort
to put an end to poverty
and to all that slowly snuffs life out
Starve he must
because you
bloated and belching
gape uncomprehendingly
at his effort
to abolish
the need and suffering
all around us

A VOICE FROM THE CHORUS.
Pausánias
Go down to the valley.
See if others have come
to join us.
Trap some game
and bring us water

PAUSÁNIAS.
And when I got there
after several
days and nights
I found Pánthea

PÁNTHEA.
And since we knew
that none were drawing near
except the executioners
dispatched from the royal barracks
and since we could already see
far off their glinting swords

we set out for
the sick man
that I might tend him
with my herbs

CHORUS.
Yet the season's winds rage
and fire falls from heaven
The parched grass burns
Frightened the peasants point
at Aetna
and well-fed armoured soldiers
are close upon the track
of the fleeing ones

PÁNTHEA.
Beside a brook
that swollen by the cloudburst
rages as it tumbles down
an arrow pierces
deep into my back
Bring him the bundle with the medicine
I call out after my friend
Don't linger

CHORUS.
The torrent bore her
to the valley where she was found
and those who came upon her saw
that this was the daughter
of Kritias the priest
and this too could be seen
as she lay shattered
that she was big with child

the son of Empedócles
O Pánthea
Pánthea the herbs you brought Empedócles
lent him
and his companions strength
so that for some few days
they stood their ground
against the mercenaries
who pressed them with
a deadly hail of missiles

HÖLDERLIN.
Pausánias falls
The farm labourers hold out
until they bleed to death.
Only one of them escapes
to spread the word
throughout the villages
of how Empedócles
eludes the enemy

A VOICE FROM THE CHORUS.
Severely wounded
in his chest and leg
dragging himself
with his last strength
across the slopes
he reaches Aetna's peak
and down he hurls himself
into that vast pit
of fire
yet leaping
he leaves behind him
wedged in a crack at the rim

a broken
iron sandal
which in the city far below
the executioners display
as if it were a sign
of victory
but is instead a sign
of their defeat

HÖLDERLIN.
For he
who never once betrayed himself
who conceded
not a single day
to the cowards
became an example
for those who will come after him.
If conditions were
unpropitious
for him and for his comrades
still we shall see
that all the slanders
the false whispers
will turn to thin air
and all that will remain
will be the actions of these few
who shall in time
become the many

*Hölderlin stands, completely exhausted. The others remain
silent. Some get up, showing signs of being stunned.*

SINGER.
Though his listeners had been open to his poetry before
they now seem struck deeply to the core

Each weighs the wasted decade since the Revolution
and none has more to say   One alone
must bear the heavy weight and silently
they step away from him   The play
however is by no means over   Consider
how young these friends here are
scarcely thirty   But age comes quickly on
The new century has just begun and Hölderlin
will live another two score years and more

Hölderlin exits quickly. A few seconds later, Sinclair follows him. Only the Chorus remains where it stood before.

SCHMID.
That he should leave in such a way and
that no mortal hand has buried him
and no man's eye has seen
his ashes

SCHELLING.
Yet formerly he could
at times be so delighted
walking the earth
and being among his fellow men
What's happened to him

GLAZIER WAGNER.
Things stand poorly with him
At night I hear him pace
for hours in his room
and although he is alone
he talks
asks questions answers them
argues with himself and screams

SCHMID.
He has drawn the line

CHORUS.
It is hard to recognize
that an act
whose sole reward is hardship
and which at first
by leaving a great emptiness
behind
appalls us
is suddenly
at work among
those it sought to reach
and sows unrest
in ever-widening circles

PÁNTHEA.
The peasant farmhands and
shepherds see
that the lords of the estates
and all their deputies
are set against them
and against them only
and that it was Empedócles
whom they let pass by
who sought to
better their lot

PAUSÁNIAS.
And in the cities
the craftsmen apprentices and
lowly tradesmen see
all around them

that it is always those
who practice usury
who cheapen
and degrade the language
whom from their palaces
the overlords protect
and that it was Empedócles
whom they let pass by
who sought to
better their lot

CHORUS.
Therefore weigh
this call
which comes from the silence
of the mountains
and put it into
words and
action

Scene 7

*Hölderlin seated on a raised platform. He is laced into
a straitjacket and wears a leather mask, which makes
him unrecognizable. An Attendant holds him tightly by the
jacket's cord. Some Students are present.*

SINGER.
Seventh scene in which
Hölderlin's face has been taken from him
and he
declared a stranger

who must become
reacquainted with himself

Enter Professor Autenrieth, director of the Tübingen
Clinic: same actor as the one who played Ephorus
Schnurrer. He taps Hölderlin's keee to test his reflexes.

SINGER.
A case of split personality is presented here
at the Tübingen Clinic The patient must wear
leather mask and jacket because he suffers from fits
during which he scratches and beats and bites
not only himself but others as well
Herr Doktor Professor Autenrieth will
examine his patient with professional skill.

Autenrieth turns to the Students.

AUTENRIETH.
With the exception of a few lucid intervals
intelligent communication with our subject has
for the past five years now
been impossible
On returning from France
in mid-July of the year eighteen hundred and two
patient arrived in a state
of mental derangement
in Stuttgart where he was treated by
Municipal Physician-in-Charge Doctor Planck
After subsiding the illness again
broke out one year thereafter and
following shorter periods of calm
became in March eighteen hundred and five
a constant condition of total insanity which
the following year

led
to his being admitted
to this our sanatorium

FIRST STUDENT.
According to the medical report
the patient was previously
capable of composing
quite pleasant verses
so the question arises
which events
unsettled his senses

AUTENRIETH.
We shall attempt
by direct address
to ascertain what remnants of
causal-coherence
remain
Observe
meanwhile his tendency
to hallucinate

Autenrieth steps back and addresses Hölderlin.

AUTENRIETH.
Friederich
Can you hear me
Friederich

Hölderlin sits up, stares ahead.

AUTENRIETH.
What drove you
to go to France

HÖLDERLIN.
Obedience Duty
diligent devoted
faithful servant
to the authorities

AUTENRIETH.
Friederich

HÖLDERLIN.
For what purpose How
destroying and darkening

AUTENRIETH.
Can you describe to us
what occurred in France

HÖLDERLIN.
The silver poplars rustle so
that grow by the Garonne
Hens cackle there
Shadowless streets and I
in my marble tomb
at Consul General Meier's

AUTENRIETH.
Patient had taken a post
as tutor with the German Consul
in Bordeaux

HÖLDERLIN.
O how the sun burned down
and the glare consumed me when
fleeing Bordeaux
I crossed the terrible Vendée
where the earth screamed of corpses

and with each step in the field
I stumbled against skulls and bones

AUTENRIETH.
Why did you leave your post

HÖLDERLIN.
The whole building split in two
The cord cut
The world shattered

AUTENRIETH.
Friederich
Can you hear me
What were you looking for
in Paris

Hölderlin leans forward, speaks tonelessly.

HÖLDERLIN.
Struck by Apollo
I found myself in the time of change
when you sense that your
way of singing takes on
another character
Stirred I went here and there
meeting many who were full of doubt
sorrow and fear and lowered their eyes
even at the sight of the madman
As I found myself in the palaces
I saw the works of antiquity
that Buonaparte had brought back
from Italy and out of Egypt the rare treasures
with which he had filled his ships
Saw all the beauty glittering before me

between the columns in the cold hall
while the prisoners rotted in the cellar
and hunger reigned in the alleys
To the sound of howling choirs
lauding the dawn of a new age
I found at the bottom of the stairs
the narrow room where
Marat's bathtub still stands in which
he was sitting when Corday
thrust the knife into his chest

AUTENRIETH.
And while there
made contact
with clandestine groups
which still stoked
the Revolution

Hölderlin leaps up.

AUTENRIETH.
Who did you see there
Tell me

Hölderlin rigidly stooped.

*Buonarotti appears. He wears a broad-brimmed hat and a
broad cloak with upturned collar.*

BUONAROTTI.
Du calme du calme
Commarade
Close yourself off
Let none know
of the Band of the Equals

AUTENRIETH.
Who do you see there

Hölderlin takes a step forward. The Attendant tightens the
leash.

BUONAROTTI.
Si brave si brave
Commarade
Don't let them drag you
to the sacrificial altar
like brother Babeuf

AUTENRIETH.
Is it Buonarroti
you see there

He raps Hölderlin's face mask.

BUONAROTTI.
Courage courage
Commarade
Keep hidden
Wait patiently
until we call you

Buonarroti vanishes.

AUTENRIETH.
Admit it
That you met
Buonarroti
and his comrades

HÖLDERLIN.
Down with all Jacobins

Vive le roi
Vive le roi

The Attendant pulls him back to the chair, shoves him down.

SECOND STUDENT.
According to his journal
immediately upon his return
patient sought out Herr Sinclair in Homburg
who stands accused of high treason

Enter Sinclair. At his side, supported by him, Susette Gontard in a long pale-violet dress, her face disfigured by a skin disease. Hölderlin, leaning forward, stares at her. All others present observe only Hölderlin, as a subject of investigation.

SUSETTE GONTARD.
I wear you see
I wear the dress
you loved so much
why have you why
hidden yourself from me
saw just now your face
your face
quickly through the bushes
come quickly
so we can take shelter o quickly
take shelter
from this storm

Hölderlin starts to whimper. The Attendant holds him firmly.

SUSETTE GONTARD.
The blood
gushes from my mouth
the blood
Where are you Holder

*Hölderlin tries to leap up. The Attendant roughly shoves
him down. Autenrieth taps his back and shoulders.*

SUSETTE GONTARD.
I'll hurry on ahead and you
run quickly up the stairs
upstairs quickly
I'll wait for you
I'll wait The door
the door as always will
as always will be open for you
the children will be studying
in the blue room then

*Hölderlin is seized with an attack of shivering. Susette
Gontard exits. Sinclair remains.*

SINCLAIR.
The object of your love is no more
I can provide no consolation
I can provide no consolation
After the winter weakened her lungs
she succumbed to her grave illness
To the very end she was true to you
To the very end she was true to you
in her thoughts remained true

*Hölderlin, shuddering, crumples. A group of Gendarmes
enters. They rush at Sinclair, throw chains over him, bind
them crosswise over him.*

AUTENRIETH.
And now it's Sinclair
that you see.
Admit it You
encouraged him
to foment revolution
in Württemberg

*Hölderlin manages to leap up. A Gendarme points at
Hölderlin.*

FIRST GENDARME.
He was there where we
found the store of weapons

AUTENRIETH.
Will you not for your own relief
confess
that you were among the conspirators
who wished to assassinate the Grand Duke

HÖLDERLIN.
I know nothing
of any conspiracy
I can stand before
His Most Gracious Excellency
the Grand Duke
with a clear conscience

AUTENRIETH.
And is Herr von Sinclair
still there

Hölderlin sobbing.

AUTENRIETH.
You recognize him

HÖLDERLIN.
Him I don't know
Him I don't know

AUTENRIETH.
You do not recognize
Court Councilor Isaac von Sinclair

HÖLDERLIN.
Him I have never
never seen him

AUTENRIETH.
So you deny knowing
your closest friend

HÖLDERLIN.
I never
had anything to do with him

AUTENRIETH.
Even as a young seminarian
you were a Jacobin

HÖLDERLIN.
I am no Jacobin
I don't want to be a Jacobin

The Attendant holds him down on the chair.

SECOND GENDARME.
This one belongs in the madhouse
and this one's headed for
prison at Hohen Asperg

They drag Sinclair off. Hölderlin singing in a high-pitched voice.

HÖLDERLIN.
O Edward o Edward
why does your shoe
so drip with blood

SINCLAIR.
O I have killed
my father dear.

Sinclair and the Gendarmes vanish.

AUTENRIETH.
And do you recall your friend
Siegfried Schmid
the true poet of the fatherland
who gave up poetry
to fight against the French

Siegfried Schmid appears, wearing a torn, mud-spattered uniform. Hölderlin shakes himself, turns away. Autenrieth and the Attendant turn him back to face forward.

A dull rumble of drums and marching.

A column of ragged soldiers marches in place. The clinking of metal.

Schmid's head and arms jerking back and forth.

SCHMID.
Napoleon leads out his rabble Leads them off to war
When they encounter the enemy rabble their orders are
slaughter them all The result's an unspeakable massacre
so many dying on the battlefield so many dead
Into our own undoing we have been led

It's those men who watch from on high in the saddle
who make history as their soldiers march into battle
at Marengo Amiens Austerlitz I was there at Marengo
not looking down from above but among the dying
    below
gun-powder smoke hanging thick in the air
and all around soldiers from everywhere
South Germans Prussians Austrians Russians
all with their own banners flags and battle cries
fighting the French All alike from the working class
It wasn't their idea to bayonet bellies to blow brains to
    bits
at Ulm and Jena and Austerlitz
I came out of it still breathing at least
but there's precious little that I haven't lost
and I'll soon die of spasms in the city of Cassel
taking leave of my life in the hospital

Schmid and the Soldiers vanish.

Holderlin once again seized with a shivering spell.

AUTENRIETH.
Now
he's trying not to imitate
his friend

Hölderlin leaps up, wailing.

HÖLDERLIN.
Basta basta

*A couple of Students and the Attendant hold Hölderlin
down. His head is pulled back. Autenrieth pours something
from a small flask into his mouth.*

AUTENRIETH.
To allay such paroxysms
we administer a mixture
of belladonna and
digitalis

Hölderlin slumps over.

Enter Hölderlin's Mother, an old woman, dressed in black.
She carries a small bundle.

HÖLDERLIN'S MOTHER
My poor little boy
I've brought you a sweater
and two pairs of stockings
but you must promise me
that you'll wear them because
I knitted them myself
You've grown so far
apart from me
and failed so bitterly
in your duty
to our dear lord
and father in heaven
If only you had listened to me
who with all my soul wished
you would pursue the clerical path
and could be settled down now
in your parish
Now I can only wait until
we meet again
in that place where there is
no parting

She holds out the bundle. Hölderlin stares at the floor. The Attendant takes the bundle.

AUTENRIETH.
You refuse then
even to recognize
your own mother

Hölderlin silent, deeply bent over.

The Mother exits.

Sinclair reappears: now without chains and guard, in the formal clothes of a princely official.

Autenrieth approaches him, greets him obsequiously.

AUTENRIETH.
Since Baron von Sinclair
has been cleared of all charges
and honorably restored
to his former high office
perhaps he may now succeed
in rousing the patient
from his stupor

SINCLAIR.
Holder
Can you hear me

Hölderlin slowly straightens.

SINCLAIR.
Holder
whenever you wish
you can return to Homburg with me
I have arranged for the count
to appoint you court librarian

Holder
I bear no grudge against you
I see in what they call
your mental derangement
a means of expression a pose
adopted for quite understandable reasons

HÖLDERLIN.
Very well Your Highness
Your Grace's gracious offer
will receive my most careful consideration

SINCLAIR.
In the meantime
it's off to France for me
to fight for Homburg's
sovereign rights

Sinclair exits.

Enter Cabinet-Maker Zimmer (same actor as the one who played Wagner). The Attendant starts to unlace Hölderlin's straitjacket.

SINGER.
At the clinic where he still sat in 1807 the doctors
whose skills had only made bad matters worse
gave the patient three years to live at most
He might have ranted and rotted until he gave up the
    ghost
if Cabinet-Maker Zimmer had not come
and taken him into his house to live with him

CABINET-MAKER ZIMMER.
I had read several poems
by the unfortunate man

that I found very much to my liking
and I thought such a great spirit
must not be allowed to go under
and perhaps I could offer this man
who so loves nature
a fine view over
the Neckar Valley

SINGER.
He would provide both bread and board.
The poet's mother for her part paid
twenty guldens a month which bought
beyond necessities tobacco wine and candlelight
by which the poet wrote at night
in the tower of the cabinet-maker's house
where in a small round room he lived out the rest of
    his days

*The Attendant has removed Hölderlin's face mask. Cabinet-
Maker Zimmer takes Hölderlin by the hand and leads him
down from the podium.*

*A couple of Students bow ironically. Hölderlin responds
with a grave bow.*

SINGER.
Johann Christian Friederich Hölderlin
before we ascend to the final scene
we hope you will explain the years-long silence
by which you kept the world at a distance
as if you no longer recognized its existence
Have you heard about Schmid and Sinclair
how they both died and for what and where
the one dreaming of a coup d'état plotted by
princes and generals the high and the mighty

the other remaining with the powerless poor
conscripted and ordered to march to war
both buried on the battlefields of their day
and the prisoners taken still not free
We'd like to know why you turned away
turned your back it would seem on the Revolution
Was it merely to mislead to escape persecution
Or was it your way of mocking your tormentors
the psyche-doctors and political mentors
Tell us Do you think you will ever again be sane
or are you condemned to crack from the strain
of expanding your thoughts to a new dimension

Hölderlin stands, reflecting. Then speaks very slowly.

HÖLDERLIN.
Would Your Eminence
grant me patience
so that I may reply
to Your Highness
as befits

SINGER.
And may I ask
the worthy Court Librarian
how long that might take

HÖLDERLIN.
Not too long.
My entire mind is bent
on said petition
and possibly as soon even
as a few years
or decades
have passed

I shall be able to
convey to Your Holiness
precisely and exhaustively
the outcome
of the working
of my thoughts

*Cabinet-Maker Zimmer exits, leading Hölderlin by the
hand.*

Scene 8

A narrow semicircle indicates the tower room.

*A couple of narrow windows, a bed-sofa, a bookshelf, a lectern-
like desk, a harpsichord.*

SINGER.
Final scene in which
Hölderlin seeks an answer
to the singer's questions and
increasingly withdraws from
our insight until a new action
breaks through to him

*Hölderlin is led in by a young girl, Christiane, the daugh-
ter of Cabinet-Maker Zimmer. (Same actress as the one
who played Fritz von Kalb and Henry Gontard.)*

*Hölderlin wears a baggy pair of knee-length breeches and a
sweat-stained, open shirt.*

SINGER.
And here we are with so much yet to tell or show
that time's passage must be compressed to flow

in a succession of fleeting moments leaving out
the endless hours We have so far in this account
depicted only one decade Now for forty years
a single room must serve within whose walls
one barely is aware of historical upheavals
It's all so calm it's hard to know for sure
if two years have just gone by or ten or more

CHRISTIANE ZIMMER.
And now the Court Librarian must
lie down here on the bed to rest
because you're tired
after our long walk

HÖLDERLIN.
Never tired
How could I be
with you to lead me
Iris
beneath the dome of heaven
beside the rivers
Open the window
Iris
See if the Ferryman
is coming

CHRISTIANE ZIMMER.
But my name isn't Iris
It's Christiane
How often do I have to tell you
And you so wise and fine
like no one else I ever knew
even though
Professor Autenrieth from the clinic says

your head is cracked
and won't get better
ever
It makes me laugh
that's all

HÖLDERLIN.
Look again
Iris
See if he's crossing
the river

Christiane opens the window, looks out.

CHRISTIANE ZIMMER.
The river is flowing quietly
and on the far shore along the quay
the seminary students
are out strolling
and no boat in sight

*Hölderlin has seated himself on the sofa. He covers his ears
with his hands.*

HÖLDERLIN.
Close the window.
The weathervane on
the seminary chapel
on the hill
crows so loud
it frightens me

CHRISTIANE ZIMMER.
Hölderlin
you should be glad
they didn't put you in the poor house

where they pack them in so tight
and where there's neither air enough nor light
so they pine away and die
abandoned and neglected

HÖLDERLIN.
You asked me
Iris
how it is out there
In the river Styx you see
the people smoulder and swell
deaf and blind and dumb
to the beauty of creation
and from the waters rise
blubb blubb
Bubbles from their mouths
blubb

He laughs raucously. Christiane sits beside him. She takes his hand.

CHRISTIANE ZIMMER.
Tell me more
about that river

HÖLDERLIN.
Okéanos flows majestic
round the earth
one branch though
plunges deep into the underworld
Where it divides in nine
there a temple rises
on the shore where
Iris
goddess of the rainbow

fetches water in a golden bowl
and sacred is this water
Woe to him who by this water
falsely swears
Yet here below
Pluto also reigns
who is so hideous
and bellows so and roars
out curses everlastingly
that it grows ever harder
for you to recognize
the truth

Hölderlin jumps up. He paces and stomps back and forth.

CHRISTIANE ZIMMER.
But the Court Librarian
must not run like that
Sit and play me something
on the harpsichord

*Hölderlin again roars with laughter. Executes a few dance
steps, grabs Christiane and swings her around. Runs then
to the harpsichord and pounds on the keyboard: a wild,
dissonant rhythm.*

*A group of Students enters, with nationalist ribbons,
rapiers, military peaked caps. They carry a basket full of
books.*

FIRST STUDENT.
People declare that he is dead
but our poet Hölderlin lives on instead
He lives up there in Zimmer's tower
creator of verses of great power

SECOND STUDENT.
Praising Germany as the chosen land
he pointed with prophetic hand
to a resplendent future because a genius
has come to lift the burden of oppression from us

THIRD STUDENT.
Hölderlin when we cross the Rhine
driving the French like a herd of swine
and march into the land of our arch foe
we'll have your odes in our backpacks when we go

Hölderlin jumps up.

HÖLDERLIN.
What's all that
howling out there

CHRISTIANE ZIMMER.
They're the young men from the student league
who've come to pay homage
to Hölderlin

The Students march on with their basket.

FIRST STUDENT.
Only the pure German spirit
shall endure
In your name Hölderlin
we deliver up
all that is foreign
to the fire

HÖLDERLIN.
What do they mean
What are they saying Iris

CHRISTIANE ZIMMER.
They've built a bonfire
in the seminary square
and are throwing on
all the books that are no good

HÖLDERLIN.
Which books then

In the glow of the flames, the Students have set down the
basket. They take books out one by one, then throw them
offstage.

FIRST STUDENT.
To protest against decadence
and the corruption of morals
Diderot

SECOND STUDENT.
We deliver up to the fire
Voltaire

THIRD STUDENT.
Rousseau

SECOND STUDENT.
In protest against insolence
and arrogance
Marat

THIRD STUDENT.
Saint Just
Robespierre

FIRST STUDENT.
We deliver up to the fire
Jacques Roux

SECOND STUDENT.
Babeuf

THIRD STUDENT.
For the glory of Hölderlin
against the mad dogs
who plot to destroy the world
through a communist
revolution
we deliver up to the fire
Buonarotti

*Sobbing, Hölderlin hides his face in his hands. The
Students exit, singing.*

THE STUDENTS.
O holy heart of the people
O German fatherland

Christiane Zimmer embraces Hölderlin.

CHRISTIANE ZIMMER.
Hölderlin
don't cry

HÖLDERLIN.
That name
I do not know that name

CHRISTIANE ZIMMER.
Calm calm
It's bad for you
to let yourself
get all excited
A little pipe-smoke
will do you good

She goes to the desk, fills a pipe, hands it to Hölderlin. She
lights the pipe. He puffs on it for a while, calms down.
Looks at the pipe.

HÖLDERLIN.
Same one that smoked for me before
when I was being taught
if nothing else
to guard this river
up there on the hill
leaning on the windowsill
and looking down upon this very tower
in which we are now
There's another one
has a trim of hammered copper
I smoked it on a hard bed
high up in the Auvergne
as I came up from Lyon through the snow
heading westward into a warm wind

He leans close to Christiane, whispers confidentially.

HÖLDERLIN.
And there's a meerschaum bowl
that comes from Frankfort
from a shop in Zeil Avenue.
O so many costly gifts
were given me

CHRISTIANE ZIMMER.
Come It's time
Court Librarian
Let's go downstairs
for supper
Father will be waiting

for you to say another
lovely grace
of far-off places
and the great god
Pan

*Holding his hand, she leads Hölderlin out. He lets himself,
suddenly stooped, be led by her.*

SINGER.
Now let another decade slip away
Hegel and Schelling arrive at last to pay
a visit to a friend whom neither man
for many years has taken time to call upon
The two philosophers had met at Karlsbad's healing
    springs
where admittedly their first few meetings
consisted of attacks on the other's theories
Yet while taking the waters and their curative ease
while worrying about their weight and maladies
each had stopped to wonder whether he
who had inspired both so generously
the poet Hölderlin was well or ill
or if he was alive at all
Thus returning to their posts by way of Tübingen
they inquired where Herr Zimmer lived and once again
beheld the seminary perched upon its hill
the silver River Neckar flowing swiftly still
and finally they knocked upon his door
whom they had last seen some thirty years before

*Holding his hand, Christiane Zimmer leads Hölderlin in.
He looks greatly aged. His clothes threadbare.*

CHRISTIANE ZIMMER.
This is the Rector of
the University in Berlin
and here from Munich
is Professor
Schelling
They have come to call upon
the honorable Court Librarian

Hölderlin, bowing deeply, retreats behind his writing desk.

HÖLDERLIN.
I humbly beg Your Majesties be seated
If your Most Gracious Royal Highness please
here on the sofa
I commend unto Your Highnesses the view
this window gives of the river which
on either side is lined with bushes
and with trees
and overhead with small white clouds

HEGEL.
Holder
don't you recognize us

HÖLDERLIN.
Venerable sir
of world-historic fame
I cannot
I may not answer that

SCHELLING.
Fritz
it is the two of us
who studied at

the seminary with you
your dear friends

HÖLDERLIN.
All things sundered
will be joined again
the glowing whole
Life is all
or so I thought
More soon

SCHELLING.
You have a fine room here
and you look very fresh and fit

CHRISTIANE ZIMMER.
Hölderle is so very well-behaved
these days and almost always
cheerful
and only rarely
has a seizure
And he writes a lot too
in his little book

HEGEL.
Would you like
to read us something
as before

Hölderlin doesn't react.

HEGEL.
Holder

SCHELLING.
Fritz
Fritz Hölderlin

CHRISTIANE ZIMMER.
He doesn't answer
to his name
You must call him
Court Librarian

HEGEL.
Would the learned Court Librarian
care to read us
from his poetry

HÖLDERLIN.
Much rather would I hear Your Awesome
and Immeasurably Elevated Majesties
tell of what occurs outside
within the great world by you
beheld understood elucidated
and stamped with your approval

HEGEL.
The Court Librarian
has doubtless heard
of the downfall and death
of the Emperor Napoleon
and of how in France
abetted by the creative impulse
of the bourgeoisie
the monarchy
has been
re-established

Hölderlin withdraws to the window. He raises his hand, speaks tonelessly.

HÖLDERLIN.
O you who with great chunks of rock
with your heavy hammers
O from out of the woods you
in carts rolling
out of the pits black
and out of the peat-bogs sweating
with axes and with spades
O out of the darkness come
and overturn the table
to which you were not invited
O turn it over
and over

Schelling turns to Christiane Zimmer.

SCHELLING.
I hope our visit
has not overwrought him

Hölderlin steps forward again.

HÖLDERLIN.
More
Tell more
Tell what other
choice events
have taken place
in the cultivated world

HEGEL.
I should sum the present
situation up thusly
The German nation while
not yet a unified state
and having been deprived

of some of its most beautiful states
is after a quarter of a century
on the way to developing
an inner strength
To be sure the wise paternal guidance
of the government
faces the impatience
of those who seek power among the people
and they endanger a harmonious becoming
The army that has been created
in an exemplary fashion
however assures that disorder shall not
fracture the foundation of the empire
Not in peace then
is the health of the state demonstrated
but only in the agitation the turmoil
of war
for the approach of whose
purifying windstorms
Friedrich Wilhelm
now prepares himself

Hölderlin roars with laughter.

HÖLDERLIN.
Friedrich Wilhelm
Friedrich Wilhelm.

HEGEL.
The monarch of Prussia.

HÖLDERLIN.
What dreadful things
come out of
the mouth of Your Magnificence

HEGEL.
Germany's task is
to regenerate the world

*Hölderlin runs to the window, jerks it open, leans out,
laughing madly.*

HÖLDERLIN.
It comes it comes
The ferry is coming closer
O breath deserts you
All you hear
are sounds of death

Schelling goes over to Hölderlin.

SCHELLING.
Fritz
I never shall forget
how you cried out
from the clouds of Aetna and
your voice was lost
in the crackling of the flames
You would break
the established orders
In your search for revelation
you broke the unity
of nature and reason
and must therefore
plunge into
chaos
Fritz
return to God
Only in the absolute principle
of the one true God

can existence
be understood
Fritz
pray
pray

Schelling on his knees, raising his hands in prayer.
Hölderlin runs to the harpsichord, pounds the keyboard
with his fists.

SCHELLING.
Fritz
Hölderlin

Hölderlin goes on pounding away.

HÖLDERLIN.
My name
Buonarroti

SCHELLING.
Wake up
Fritz
Reject the sacrificial death
Who is helped
if you broil in the crater
Who is helped by the smoke
of your bones
Remain
at the foot of the mountain
among those
who need you

Hölderlin pounding away.

HÖLDERLIN.
Killalusimono
Killalusimono
Nothing is happening to me
Nothing is happening to me

SCHELLING.
Dear friend
Come to your senses
Listen to us

Hölderlin shoves him away, continues with the hammering. Christiane strokes Hölderlin's head, gradually calms him.

Schelling and Hegel slowly back away. After a moment Christiane takes Hölderlin's hand and leads him off.

SINGER.
Skip quickly now to eighteen hundred forty-three
the last year of his life in which he cheerfully
returns from hill and meadow and from country lane
to that garden house whose tower golden in the sun
rises by the Neckar where the river bends
hard by the bridge and then serenely wends
its way from Tübingen with its castle and seminary
to flow through meadow lands and open country

Hölderlin is led in by the hand by Lotte Zimmer, Christiane's younger sister (played by the same actress as the one who played Christiane). Hölderlin deeply stooped. Walks with difficulty.

SINGER.
Although it may appear that he's still led
by Christiane Zimmer untouched by age it is instead

so that those who pride themselves on thinking logically
    may know
her younger sister who now helps him to and fro
Her name is Lotte yet for the poet she
is Iris as her sister was and he trusts in her implicitly

Hölderlin stops, raises a hand, speaks very softly.

HÖLDERLIN.
You are I know beyond my reach
for the sight of you
comes to me from another life
yet you appear here now
as if you still remain
even for me in my long decline

LOTTE ZIMMER.
Does the Court Librarian know
that a visitor awaits him

Hölderlin grows restless, retreats to his desk.

LOTTE ZIMMER.
Now now
There's no cause to be upset
He is he says
a great admirer
of your poetry
and writes himself and is
the editor
of the *Rheinische Zeitung*

*Enter the young Karl Marx. He stands, waiting. Hölderlin
bows deeply.*

HÖLDERLIN.
Assume Your Highness knows
my having-becomeness
and humbly I appreciate
grateful for notice paid
my me and not-me
Have no other way to say

He starts to whistle.

LOTTE ZIMMER.
Please don't look at this
as a sign of madness
It's his weakness
that brings it out in him

MARX.
I've heard Court Librarian
that you like me
enjoy a smoke
so I've brought some tobacco
Even though it's a brand
made by the thievish English
it makes for an agreeable
smoke

*From his pocket, Marx takes out a big packet of tobacco,
holds it out to Hölderlin. Since Hölderlin does not reach
out for it, Lotte Zimmer takes it, carries it to the desk and
fills a pipe.*

Marx also takes out a pipe.

*Lottle hands Hölderlin the filled pipe. Marx offers him a
light, then lights his own pipe. For a few moments, both
smoke. Marx starts to laugh.*

MARX.
It was my encounter
with your works
and more especially with *Hyperion*
that with one blow
shattered all my own attempts
Faced with such light
such clarity
my own scribblings
crumbled to
nothing
You most honored sir
made life very hard for me
for suddenly I saw
that all I took for poetry
had been constructed on the moon
And then
as all that fell away
with all that I had aimed at
a hazy notion of some great beyond
I tried
to put myself together again
New gods had to take the place of old
within the shattered sanctuary

Hölderlin has stepped closer to Marx. He listens closely.

MARX.
If formerly the gods
had dwelt above the earth
now they had become
its core
The infinite was abolished
and in its place there stood

the finite and
the real
You
from an elevated vantage
managed to catch and mirror
an entire epoch
What I did was to set to work
as I pursued my studies in philosophy
and law
to examine the conditions
in which men live
Burrowing deeply into the laws
of private property
I saw thievery
and plundering orgies
of betrayal and corruption
of cold-blooded murder
by means of which
our social system
had achieved its splendour

HÖLDERLIN.
Not so fast please.
Slower
so I can follow
Your Noble Grace
I live at the very threshold
of the grave
Ready any moment
to go if called
Has also been great strain
to hold out here
on the far side
of the inhabited world

MARX.
Two paths can be taken
to prepare the way
for fundamental change
One is
the analysis of the concrete
historical situation
The other
the visionary formulation
of deepest personal experience

HÖLDERLIN.
And yet
however

MARX.
I submit to you
that both paths are
equally valid.
That you
some fifty years ago
should describe the Revolution
not as scientifically based
necessity
but as a premonition
embodied in a myth
is not your fault

Hölderlin speaks slowly, searching for words.

HÖLDERLIN.
Now one comes here
into this room
which since the War
of Liberation was fought in Greece

has not removed
its outer shutters
and for the first time I can hear
for I was deeply sunk
in contemplation of the wounded
and the slain
how a voice
resounding in my ear
recalls itself
within me

A moment of silence.

MARX.
I looked in vain
through all the respected
Court Librarian's works
brought out by Cotta
for a tragedy you wrote
whose theme as I was told
concerns an armed uprising

Holderlin, eagerly, agitated.

HÖLDERLIN.
You say so
you assert so
and so Your Highness
there must be truth
in what you say
because it treats
perhaps of Spartacus
the slave who dared rise up
against the procurators or

of Babeuf whom
I was close to in the Band of Equals

He hurries to the desk, shuffles restlessly through papers.
Marx waits patiently.

But Hölderlin appears to have forgotten what he was
looking for. He stands motionless at the desk, starts to
whistle again.

MARX.
When you took up your task
there were as yet none
capable of listening to you
and responding
Impossible for a single man
to tear up
the entire tightly woven web

HÖLDERLIN.
Many
There were many

MARX.
Even the most level-headed
the most persevering remained
trapped within their origins
could not cross over
from the democratic ground
to the proletarian element.

Hölderlin starts to speak again, then can't continue. Marx
waits.

HÖLDERLIN.
O the blinding brightness
in this room

Imagine it as breaking in
upon the dreamer
in deepest darkness
And this stillness
inconceivable
how much of it
as if crashing out in thunder
has accumulated from remotest time
until the coming day
Full stop

Silence

MARX.
When in Paris
rebellion broke out
four decades after the Bastille fell
Buonarroti
took part in it once more
before he died
in exile
destitute
forgotten
the workers crushed
the power of the financiers
secured anew
And yet you see
suddenly his words
are heard again
among the workers
now gathering in Paris
for the assault

*Hölderlin again shuffles through his papers. He pulls out a
sheaf of manuscript pages. Talks excitedly, in a rush.*

HÖLDERLIN.
Here
They refused
when I stand on the steps
of the theater in Weimar
these roles which I have
written down freely
after Sophocles and Virgil
to rehearse and
prepare for production
Could you see to it
that the duke
order the actors
to appear at once
only

He steps close to Marx, whispers.

HÖLDERLIN.
Only
Privy Counselor Goethe
must not know of this

MARX.
Goethe is dead

HÖLDERLIN.
Nor Herr von Schiller
either

MARX.
He's dead

HÖLDERLIN.
And Fichte

MARX.
He's dead too

Hölderlin in great excitement returns to his desk, searches through his papers.

HÖLDERLIN.
Then I will have a copy
written out at once
Now finally we can
move forward
The doors at last
stand open

Clutching an armful of manuscript pages, he leaps down-stage, some pages falling to the floor. For a while he stands there confused, then slowly turns, goes to the sofa, sits. He remains seated like this, the pages in his lap.

Lotte Zimmer opens the windows.

Since Hölderlin does not look up again, Marx withdraws from him.

LOTTE ZIMMER.
He's tired now
He must sleep now
You'll pardon me
Herr Marx
if I show you out

Lotte Zimmer and Marx exit slowly.
Hölderlin motionless.

Epilogue

*Enter Hegel, Hiller (-Schmid), Neuffer, Schelling, Sinclair
dressed as at the beginning of the play. They carry garlands
and wreaths. The Singer leads Hölderlin forward.*

All arrange themselves in the tableau of an apotheosis.

Joining them, the Male and Female Workers.

SINGER.
Epilogue

HÖLDERLIN.
True you can find words I left behind that extol
improvement and renewal or that tell
how I loved the specific and the singular
in an age when generalities were the rule
Still try as I might I could not maintain
a balance between the power without and that within
The Revolution as an ideal was so real to me
that I was shattered by what happened in reality
a ghastly prison-world rose up in place of paradise
the promised world could not be recognized
The overwhelming powers of the time left me no choice
but to keep silent a poet who had lost his voice

ALL.
And remained so for half of your long life
preferring to live apart aloof
than to re-enter a world torn by strife

HÖLDERLIN.
We have presented the form of Hölderlin in such a way
that he finds himself within the play
and acting as if he not only mirrors bygone days
but wrestles with the problems that we face

or rack our brains searching for solutions
to them or attempting to revolve life's contradictions
His wish is that he be seen as who he is
not one who dives headlong into the fiery abyss
but as one among the many of his day who chose
through language and through art to express themselves
Nor would he consider dreams
as separate from reality nor assign to different rooms
fantasy and action For only if they live together
each enriching one another
can the poetic become universal
strong enough to do battle with all
that's stale and ossified and dull
and that by using threats and violence
would squeeze the very air out of our existence
Never again will he vanish in silent separation
but will enter the circle of living voices alive again

The tableau dissolves.

SINGER.
After he sank out of sight and lay under the turf
even after his body had turned to earth
and only the gravestone at his head
showed he had lived and the year he died
his prison stood on the bank of the Neckar
Even today you can see it standing there

—Revised version: December 1971–April 1972

AFTERWORD

While in the staging of the play no attempt whatsoever should be made to present the characters in a portrait-likeness, the following characteristics may be useful in shaping some of the leading roles. Hölderlin's contemporaries described him as tall and beautiful, but this should not lead to his appearing first as a youthful hero and later as the Great Solitary. The eccentric and tragic nature of the figure should not be accentuated. His gradually increasing isolation should not be presented as a consequence of his genius, his originality, but as a fundamentally involuntary response to a predicament imposed by society. Hölderlin is not the only one presented as being in this specific historical situation: all those around him are caught up in it, each in his own way, and those who suffer most are the representatives of the rural population, who have been almost completely robbed of the means of expressing themselves.

His psychological vulnerability should not be exploited to give the impression of an eccentric, psychopathic character in whom the later decline is foreshadowed from the start—rather what should be brought out is that, despite the defeats that he must suffer, he never abandons his belief in a better future.

He is not a sufferer in the usual use of the term; his temperament is seismographic. His openness, his vitality are of an unusual order, but what does affect him does so because he represents a type of individual who has been cast out and driven into a corner by his epoch. The less he is defined by individual misfortune and individual decline, the more strongly he can serve as manifestation of the contradictions, the turmoil of the time.

The role is best structured by working backward from the conclusion: the aging Hölderlin lived in his tower for 40 years, outliving most of his friends and opponents—a striking metaphor for the patience and hopes that persist beneath the spiritual darkening.

HEGEL is Hölderlin's principal opponent. There is great understanding between the two. They have learned from each other, have enriched each other, and when Hegel attacks Hölderlin, he does so as a friend. Nevertheless, Hegel's basic attitude, so intrinsically different from Hölderlin's, must in the end find expression as a position from which there is no bridge to Hölderlin's ideas. He would like to be able to effect a change in Hölderlin. He sees the danger in Hölderlin's life. He wishes that his friend would keep to the possible, in line with his own prescription of the ideal—to be a man of reason, who understands how to adapt to the conditions of reality. Essentially, however, Hegel lives in an abstract intellectual world, and when we compare his world with Hölderlin's, we find that he, although successful, installed as a professor, as a university rector, in no way shows a deeper grasp of reality than Hölderlin in his hymnic visions.

Still, in his bearing, he always appears stronger, more persuasive than Hölderlin, and perhaps he gains in stature as a foil to Hölderlin's more fluid, wide-open sensibility.

Hegel is sharp and clear in his speech, and at times somewhat lecturing, but not without humor.

SCHELLING has none of Hegel's persuasiveness. He always comes across as honest, was doubtless an enthusiastic supporter of revolutionary ideals as a youth, but is in the end always a follower, facile and smooth, for whom finally nothing is left but traditional faith in God. In him the romantic, the irrational come to the fore, which at times influenced Hölderlin's view of the world, imposed on him his utopian views and impulses to escape from the concrete into the mystical eternal.

In the course of his development into a highly respected citizen—he keeps up his old friendship with Hölderlin—yet he increasingly demonstrated to him that he was the one who knows better. He makes sure that the derailed poet knows that he has Goethe's support and that he holds the post in Jena which the great minds and powers that be denied to Hölderlin.

NEUFFER retains, alongside his duties as preacher, his love of poetry, and continues to regard himself as a poet rather than as a priest. Not denying himself worldly pleasures and full of understanding for the exigencies of everyday life, he has great affection for Hölderlin, so rootless and repeatedly headed for the edge of the abyss. With his warm and naïve nature, he is closer to Hölderlin than Schelling and Hegel can bring themselves to be. His relationship to Hölderlin is one that is almost tender, the sort that in those days was expressed in embraces and kisses.

SINCLAIR, as hinted at in the ballad 'O Edward', was of noble Scottish descent, and Hölderlin admired him because of his bold, fiery character. But it is doubtful that Sinclair closely resembled the figure that Hölderlin depicted in many poems. Despite his radical nature, his willingness to suffer every penalty for his convictions, he always retained a certain opacity—a characteristic which he later, in his profession as diplomat, also understood how to employ. As a tyrannicide he remains a poetical figure, and because so little biographical material about him has survived, we can take the liberty of letting him appear as Hölderlin saw him—as a demigod. But it should not be forgotten that his co-conspirators on the highest political level do not support an uprising by the masses, but a coup from above, and that his Jacobinic ideals were shaped by the interests of an educated elite. It is precisely because of his privileged position that Hölderlin, with his unrealistic tendency, is able to transform him into an antique mythological hero.

Sinclair, for his part, despite the courtly circle in which he moves, never forgets to step in for his socially less-accomplished friend, even at a time when catastrophe crashes down on him. The fact that he takes him in, finds him a position as librarian in the castle of the landgrave, is a sign of his admiration of the poet, whose unwillingness to compromise and whose linguistic creativity have made a deep impression on him.

But even if Hölderlin found understanding and devotion among his closest circle of friends—a fact that could compensate for the scathing official criticism—a break between his world and the world of his friends was in the end unavoidable. Even Sinclair eventually cannot penetrate the profound isolation into which Hölderlin descends. But while Hegel, Schelling, and Neuffer suppress thoughts of the prisoner, it is safe to assume that Sinclair, during his last years in the diplomatic service, preserved the image of his friend and his view of the world.

SCHMID remained closely connected with Hölderlin to the very end. Physically and mentally battered on battlefields and in hospitals, he appears as a figure who, under the force of the events of his time, erases all traces of himself and so takes the same path that puts Hölderlin in the tower and into endless exile. Schmid, in his helplessness, his inability to find a suitable means of expressing his restless aimless existence, neither intellectually nor poetically particularly gifted, but full of strong reactions against the oppressive mechanisms of his time, stands virtually anonymous for many others who have nothing but their lives to offer, and their impatient hope for social renewal.

Schmid is close to the anonymous farmhands, servants, and maids, who from time to time make their appearances and, in the form of popular and satirical songs, express the indignation welling up in the population, without yet coming together to form a common cause.

These workers, male and female, should, although they appear only sporadically to form a leitmotif, be presented with great clarity and conviction. For they, although constituting only a small group here, represent the great majority of the people who, otherwise, in the midst of all the poets and thinkers assembled in this play, are barely mentioned.

Because this play is concerned, above all, with the general structure of society and its effects on some of the most significant personalities in art and science, the entrances of the workers should strongly suggest the foundation that supports the society.

GOETHE, short, stocky, sturdy, erect of posture, is conscious of his position as leading intellectual and humanist. With his universal spirit, he is open, like no other, to the possibilities of development, the tensions, and the crises of his time, but he also knows how to provide a counterbalance of equanimity to all that is unsettling and destructive.

Hölderlin, full of impatience after his year in Waltershausen, full of revolt against the barriers that would restrict his artistic development, is confronted with Goethe's monumental stability. The realism and positivism in Goethe's nature lead to an aversion to those artists most affected by the problems and conflicts of the time. Just as reason has him protest against destabilization of the social order, so too he condemns a poetry that clashes with his image of what is bright, unified, and confident and that sounds notes of complicated and confused emotions. It was not only to Hölderlin that he exhibited this antipathy—he also rejected Novalis and Kleist.

To be sure, he welcomed the Revolution of 1789, but only as a step toward self-liberation of the citizen. Every act of violence driven by the power of the people is, to him, repugnant. On the other hand, in his esteem of all that is authoritarian, he sees the Napoleonic imperium as the rightful successor of the Revolution.

He supports social improvement leading to reform. He believes in evolution through education and instruction— the misery, the filth, the hunger of the fourth estate that continued to be oppressed, meanwhile, remain remote to him. Even Schiller's play *Die Räuber* (The Robbers) seemed suspect to him, inasmuch as it exhibited something of the wild power of the lower classes. It was only when Schiller distanced himself from unruliness and embraced aesthetic and pedagogic values that he drew close to him. Yet certain reservations regarding Schiller remained—hints of this attitude can be expressed in the Jena scene.

While Goethe's superiority, seen from Hölderlin's point of view, takes on exaggerated, distorted features, the privy counselor, deeply rooted in the middle class, should not be caricatured.

The more positive the presentation of Goethe, the more pronounced and merciless the clash that emerges between two worlds, a clash that will destroy Hölderlin.

SCHILLER, big, gaunt, sickly, coughing. A lung ailment and stomach pains often make it hard for him to hold himself erect. One has the impression that much of what Schiller says is intended for Goethe to hear rather than Hölderlin. Schiller understands Hölderlin's uniqueness, but he is almost compulsively driven to find fault with Hölderlin's poetics, solely in order to align himself with Goethe's standards. This is what gives him, despite his intensity, his high flights of thought, a certain air of the schoolmaster.

For Hölderlin, Goethe's liberal progressive stance is a formidable obstacle; for Schiller, the highest maturity. In his ambitious need to gain Goethe's respect and to work with him to establish a national culture, Schiller slips easily into a submissive manner, which leads to a bit of mockery and condescension on Goethe's part.

Viewed against Goethe's quiet self-assurance, Schiller's tragedy becomes evident—he tries too hard to make himself into a literary educator; he reins himself in, suppresses his recognition of social injustices, forces himself to adopt a noble restraint.

What, in fact, he should say to Hölderlin is: You're on the right path. Do what you feel you need to. Make real your dreams. But in Goethe's presence, the petit-bourgeois citizen in him wins out over his original inclination, which is to play a direct role in changing social conditions.

FICHTE becomes the spokesman for the whole German dilemma. He, who theoretically fully supports the necessity of revolution and does not reject the use of force, shies away from the direct practical application of his teaching. Aware that his preconditions for revolution have not yet been met, he has the right objections to his own thesis ready at hand. but one cannot help but feel that, even if the people were ripe for revolt, he would shrink from the decisive revolutionary act.

It is painful, then, to see how, later, his well-intentioned calls for change are twisted by the nationalist mentality, even to the point of proving useful in supporting fascism.

HEINRICH VON KALB sits there in his muddy boots. He, the landed junker, dreams of armies advancing in far corners of the world. He is a colonialist before his country had reached the imperialist stage. He is not comfortable in the presence of his women, and even lets his estate fall into disrepair. All his big talk cannot hide the fact that he is, essentially, a broken man. Soon his property will have deteriorated to such a degree that he will have no choice but to put a bullet in his head. The tales he tells his son about the Wild West cannot compensate for the beatings he has already inflicted on the boy. In his house, everything is going to ruin—this makes the idyll, with music and drinks, seem eerie and ghostly. In Waltershausen the last remnants of feudalism are rotting.

CHARLOTTE VON KALB dulls her sense of being lost with wine. In her, too, a certain sloppiness has set in, although she retains traces of her former beauty. Her literal myopia, which has rendered her almost blind, magnifies the helplessness of her situation. Her manner of cautiously feeling her way about the room can suggest the downfall of her class—but without symbolism, just a dreary and inevitable deterioration.

WILHELMINE KIRMS, within this milieu, is the representative of a future emancipation. But she should not, by any means, be presented as a blue stocking—she is modern, progressive, extremely attractive. When she makes advances to Hölderlin, there is no awkwardness. Her directness is natural to her. When she bares her breast, she does not do so to the public—the gesture has nothing of the sensational about it, but only the intimacy toward the man, whom she would like to have as a partner. Set against her matter-of-factness, all that is unresolved in Hölderlin's being is thrust more sharply into relief. Her tone, which in the Empedócles scene, where she takes the part of Pánthea, reaches its full climax, is already suggested in Waltershausen.

SUSETTE GONTARD, another victim of her class. Her love for Hölderlin is platonic. For her, owned as it were by the upper-class master, there is no possibility of escape. She can find a place to relate to Hölderlin, her house servant and house poet, only in a hysterically exaggerated dream world. Her love may be genuine, just as Hölderlin is consumed with longing for her, but having lived a lie has cast such a shadow that each word, each gesture, each risk of embrace, immediately brings with it such a threat of punishment that finally everything goes up in flames of madness.

Undoubtedly the year-long agony of this unconsummated attraction contributed to Hölderlin's collapse—the brief *Totentanz* entrances and exits of the Frankfurt garden party should demonstrate how the physical existence of the lovers is tortured, beaten, and torn apart by the economic overlords.

The CHORUS in the Empedócles scene consists of the workers, male and female, to show whom Hölderlin now selects for his central theme. In his drafts of the tragedy *The Death of Empedócles*, Hölderlin frequently indicates the significance he attributes to the Chorus of the People, the Delegates of the People.

After his exhausting passage through the bourgeois machine, which has nothing more to offer him than the madhouse and, finally, exile in the tower, he now faces those whom he sees 'in their true form, as they mirror themselves in him, whose death is his love, his sincerity, in an effort to bind him to themselves'—as he noted at the end of the draft of the third revision. In dealing with the Chorus, which his friends continue to challenge with arguments of the conformists, his wish to reach those 'with the pure look/the open ear' is fulfilled.

Translated by Jon Swan, with Ingrid MacGillis